W9-DII-142

Mastering Math is designed to help children reinforce and develop mathematical skills. There are numerous exercises that enable children to practice problems dealing with fractions, decimals, graphs, and measurement as well as addition, subtraction, and multiplying with two- and three-digit numbers. Children also are introduced to division, rounding, and estimating. The Mastering Math system is designed for independent study.

Table Of Contents

Glossary

Angle. Two rays with the same end point.

Area. The number of square units needed to cover a region.

Centimeter. A metric system measurement. There are 2.54 centimeters in an inch.

Cup (c.). A unit of volume in the customary system equal to 8 ounces.

Decimal. A number with one or more places to the right of a decimal point, such as 6.5 or 2.25.

Denominator. The number below the fraction bar in a fraction.

Diameter. A line segment that passes through the center of a circle and has both end points on the circle.

Digit. The symbols used to write numbers: 0, 1, 2, 3, 4, 5, 6, 7, 8, and 9.

Dividend. The larger number that is divided by the smaller number, or divisor, in a division problem. In the problem 28 ÷ 7 = 4, 28 is the dividend.

Divisor. The number that is divided into the dividend in a division problem. In the problem 28 ÷ 7 = 4, 7 is the divisor.

Equivalent Fractions. Fractions that name the same number.

Estimate. To give an approximate rather than an exact answer.

Factor. The numbers multiplied together in a multiplication problem.

Fraction. A number that names part of a whole, such as 1/2 or 1/3.

Kilometer (km). A unit of length. There are 1000 meters in a kilometer.

Liter (L). A unit in the metric system used to measure amounts of liquid.

Meter (m). A unit of length in the metric system. A meter is equal to 39.37 inches.

Mile (mi.). A mile is equal to 1760 yards.

Mixed Numeral. A number written as a whole number and a fraction.

Multiple. The product of a specific number and any other number. For example, the multiples of 2 are 2 (2 x 1), 4 (2 x 2), 6, 8, 10, 12, and so on.

Numerator. The number above the fraction bar in a fraction.

Octagon. A polygon with eight sides.

Ordered Pair. A pair of numbers used to locate a point in a plane.

Pentagon. A polygon with five sides.

Perimeter. The distance around an object. Found by adding the lengths of the sides.

Pint (pt). A unit of volume in the customary system equal to 2 cups.

Polygon. A closed plane figure with straight sides called line segments.

Product. The answer of a multiplication problem.

Quart (qt). A unit of volume equal to four cups or two pints.

Quotient. The answer of a division problem.

Radius. A line segment with one endpoint on the circle and the other end point at the center.

Rectangle. A figure with four corners and four sides. Sides opposite each other are the same length.

Regroup. To use one ten to form ten ones, one 100 to form ten tens, fifteen ones to form one ten and five ones, and so on.

Remainder. The number left over in the quotient of a division problem.

Rounding. Expressing a number to the nearest ten, hundred, thousand, and so on. For example, round 18 up to 20; round 11 down to 10.

Sequencing. Putting numbers in the correct order, such as 7, 8, 9.

Square. A figure with four corners and four sides of the same length.

Triangle. A figure with three corners and three sides.

Yard. A measurement of distance in the customary system. There are three feet in a yard.

Name: _____

Place Value

Place value is the value of a digit, or numeral, shown by where it is in the number. For example, in the number 1234, 1 has the place value of thousands, 2 is hundreds, 3 is tens, and 4 is ones.

Directions: Put the numbers in the correct boxes to find how far the car has traveled.

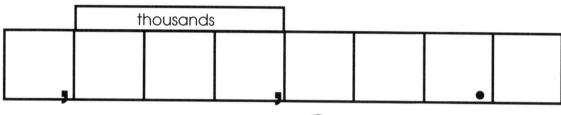

one thousand
six hundreds
eight ones
nine ten thousands
four tens
two millions
seven tenths
five hundred thousands

How many miles has the car traveled? _____

Directions:

In the number:

2386	_____ is in the ones place.
4957	_____ is in the hundreds place.
102,432	_____ is in the ten thousands place.
489,753	_____ is in the one thousands place.
1,743,998	_____ is in the millions place.
9,301,671	_____ is in the hundred thousands place.
7,521,834	_____ is in the tens place.

Name: _____

Addition

Addition is "putting together" or adding two or more numbers to find the sum. Regrouping is to use one ten to form ten ones, one 100 to form ten tens, fifteen ones to form one ten and five ones, and so on.

Directions: Add using regrouping. Color in all of the boxes with a 5 in the answer to help the dog find its way home.

	63 +22	5268 4910 +1683	248 +463	291 +543	2934 +112
1736 +5367	2946 +7384	3245 1239 +981	738 +692	896 +729	594 +738
2603 +5004	4507 +289	1483 +6753	1258 +6301	27 469 +6002	4637 +7531
782 +65	485 +276	3421 +8064			
48 93 +26	90 263 +864	362 453 +800			

4

Name: _____

Subtraction

Subtraction is "taking away" or subtracting one number from another. Regrouping is to use one ten to form ten ones, one 100 to form ten tens, fifteen ones to form one ten and five ones, and so on.

Directions: Subtract using regrouping.

Examples:

$$\begin{array}{r} 23 \\ -18 \\ \hline 5 \end{array}$$

$$\begin{array}{r} 243 \\ -96 \\ \hline 147 \end{array}$$

$$\begin{array}{r} 81 \\ -53 \\ \hline \end{array} \qquad \begin{array}{r} 76 \\ -49 \\ \hline \end{array} \qquad \begin{array}{r} 94 \\ -38 \\ \hline \end{array} \qquad \begin{array}{r} 156 \\ -77 \\ \hline \end{array} \qquad \begin{array}{r} 243 \\ -29 \\ \hline \end{array} \qquad \begin{array}{r} 468 \\ -293 \\ \hline \end{array}$$

$$\begin{array}{r} 341 \\ -83 \\ \hline \end{array} \qquad \begin{array}{r} 568 \\ -173 \\ \hline \end{array} \qquad \begin{array}{r} 806 \\ -738 \\ \hline \end{array} \qquad \begin{array}{r} 647 \\ -289 \\ \hline \end{array} \qquad \begin{array}{r} 730 \\ -518 \\ \hline \end{array} \qquad \begin{array}{r} 961 \\ -846 \\ \hline \end{array}$$

$$\begin{array}{r} 573 \\ -76 \\ \hline \end{array} \qquad \begin{array}{r} 604 \\ -55 \\ \hline \end{array} \qquad \begin{array}{r} 254 \\ -69 \\ \hline \end{array} \qquad \begin{array}{r} 111 \\ -82 \\ \hline \end{array} \qquad \begin{array}{r} 358 \\ -99 \\ \hline \end{array} \qquad \begin{array}{r} 147 \\ -49 \\ \hline \end{array}$$

$$\begin{array}{r} 265 \\ -19 \\ \hline \end{array} \qquad \begin{array}{r} 372 \\ -59 \\ \hline \end{array} \qquad \begin{array}{r} 180 \\ -106 \\ \hline \end{array} \qquad \begin{array}{r} 325 \\ -68 \\ \hline \end{array} \qquad \begin{array}{r} 873 \\ -35 \\ \hline \end{array} \qquad \begin{array}{r} 726 \\ -29 \\ \hline \end{array}$$

Name: Thomas Graham

Rounding

Rounding a number means expressing it to the nearest ten, hundred, thousand, and so on.

Directions: Round the following numbers to the nearest ten. If the number has 5 ones or more, round it up to the next highest ten. For example, round 26 up to 30. If the number has 4 ones or less, round down to the nearest ten, such as rounding 44 down to 40.

18 __20__   33 __30__   82 __80__   56 __60__

24 __20__   49 __50__   91 __90__   67 __70__

Directions: Round to the nearest hundred. If 5 tens or more, round up. If 4 tens or less, round down.

243 __200__   689 __700__   263 __300__   162 __200__

389 __400__   720 __700__   351 __400__   490 __500__

463 __500__   846 __800__   928 __900__   733 __700__

Directions: Round to the nearest thousand. If number has 5 hundreds or more, round up. If 4 hundreds or less, round down.

2638 __3000__   3940 __4000__   8653 __9000__   6238 __6000__

1429 __1000__   5061 __5000__   7289 __7000__   2742 __3000__

9460 __9090__   3109 __3000__   4697 __5000__   8302 __8000__

Directions: Round to the nearest ten thousand. If the number has 5 thousands or more, round up. If 4 thousands or less, round down.

11,368 __10,000__   38,421 __40,000__   75,302 __80,000__   67,932 __70,000__

14,569 __10,000__   49,926 __50,000__   93,694 __90,000__   81,648 __80,000__

26,784 __30,000__   87,065 __90,000__   57,843 __60,000__   29,399 __30,000__

Name: _____

Addition And Subtraction

Addition is "putting together" or adding two or more numbers to find the sum. Subtraction is "taking away" or subtracting one number from another.

Regrouping is to use one ten to form ten ones, one 100 to form ten tens, fifteen ones to form one ten and five ones, and so on.

Directions: Add or subtract. Remember to regroup.

```
   32        183        456        643
   68        246        398       -377
  +43        +89       +597


 1563       3586       8711       9361       5734
 -941      +4218      -4937      -7452      +6298


  293        743        849       1227       9117
  431       -529        250       2431      -3828
  +93                   +82      +5792
```

58 + 93 + 146 = _____   73 + 246 + 1579 = _____

43 + 745 - 29 = _____   128 + 403 + 2571= _____

156 + 627 + 541 = _____   97 + 51 + 37 + 79 = _____

Tom walks 389 steps from his house to the video store. It is 149 steps to Elm Street. It is 52 steps from Maple Street to the video store. How many steps is it from Elm Street to Maple Steet?

_____

Name: _____

Addition And Subtraction

Addition is "putting together" or adding two or more numbers to find the sum. Subtraction is "taking away" or subtracting one number from another.

Directions: Add or subtract.

38	1269	5792	629	4697
43	2453	-4814	491	-2988
+21	+8219		+308	

5280	68	197	7321	456
-3147	27	436	-2789	+974
	+42	+213		

3932	492	9873	4978	6235
+4681	863	+5483	+2131	+2986
	+57			

Sue stocked her pond with 263 bass and 187 trout. The turtles ate 97 fish. How many fish are left? _____

Name: _____

Multiples

A multiple is the product of a specific number and any other number. For example, the multiples of 2 are 2 (2 x 1) 4, (2 x 2), 6, 8, 10, 12, and so on.

Directions: Write the missing multiples.

Example: Count by fives.
5, 10, 15, 20, 25, 30, 35. These are multiples of 5.

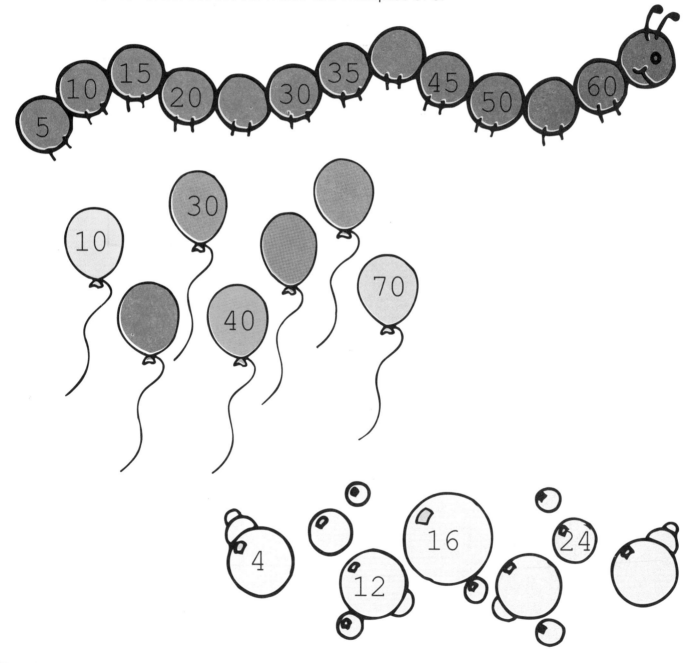

Name: _____

Review

Directions: Add or subtract using regrouping.

67 93 +48	5029 -3068	732 801 +18	2467 +3184	8453 -6087
5792 -3889	7489 +5938	463 -209	3537 -2394	6342 +959

Directions: Write the numbers in the boxes.

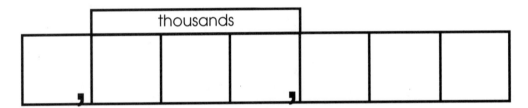

eight million, four hundred thousand, nine hundred fifty two

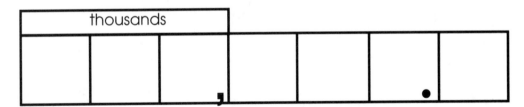

five hundred thousands, three ten thousands, five thousands, zero hundreds, four tens, one one, two tenths

Directions: Fill in the blanks with the missing multiples.

6, 12, 18, _____, 30, _____

4, _____, 12, 16, _____, 24

3, _____, _____, 12, 15

_____, 10, 15, _____, _____

Multiplication

to problems is maintain

Multiplication is a short way to find the sum of adding the same number a certain amount of times, such as 7 x 4 = 28 instead of 7 + 7 + 7 + 7 = 28.

Directions: Multiply as fast as you can.

4	7	0	
x7	x6	x8	
28	42	0	

7	9	1	6
x2	x5	x5	x4
14	45	5	27

8	7	4	9
x3	x1	x2	x6
24	7	8	54

8	6	9	3	7
x5	x7	x8	x5	x8
40	42	72	15	56

3	5	9	7	9
x9	x6	x9	x5	x4
27	30	84	35	36

3	2	8	7
x6	x8	x6	x7
18	16	48	49

0	3	5
x7	x3	x9
0	9	45

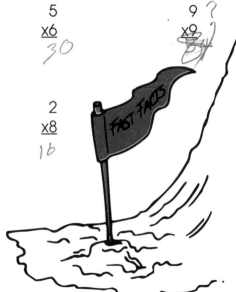

FAST FACTS

11

Name: _____

Multiplication: Tens, Hundreds, And Thousands

Multiplication is a short way to find the sum of adding the same number a certain amount of times, such as 7 x 4 = 28 instead of 7 + 7 + 7 + 7 = 28.

Directions: Study the examples.

Examples:

When multiplying a number by 10, the answer is the number with a zero.
It is like counting by 10s.

10	10	10	10	10	10
x1	x2	x3	x4	x5	x6
10	20	30	40	50	60

When multiplying a number by 100, the answer is the number with two zeroes.
When multiplying a number by 1000, the answer is the number with three zeroes.

100	100	100	1000	1000	1000
x1	x2	x3	x1	x2	x3
100	200	300	1000	2000	3000

Such basic facts help us multiply.

4	400	8	800	7	700
x2	x2	x3	x3	x5	x5
8	800	24	2400	35	3,500

Directions: Multiply.

10	60	400	700	50
x3	x5	x5	x8	x7

80	4000	6000	300	700
x9	x2	x4	x9	x6

3 x 800 = _____   9 x 2000 = _____   7 x 90 = _____

Name: _____

Multiplication: One-Digit Number x Two-Digit Number

Multiplication is a short way to find the sum of adding the same number a certain amount of times, such as 7 x 4 = 28 instead of 7 + 7 + 7 + 7 = 28.

Directions: Study the example. Follow the steps to multiplying by regrouping tens.

Example:

Step 1. Multiply ones. Regroup.

```
 54
 x7
  8
```

Step 2. Multiply Tens. Add 2 tens.

```
 54
 x7
378
```

```
 27        63        52        91        45
 x3        x4        x5        x9        x7
```

```
 75        64        76        93        87
 x2        x5        x3        x6        x4
```

```
 66        38        47        64        51
 x7        x2        x8        x9        x8
```

```
 99        13        32        25        15
 x3        x7        x4        x8        x7
```

The chickens on the Smith farm produce 48 dozen eggs each day.
How many dozen eggs do they produce in 7 days?

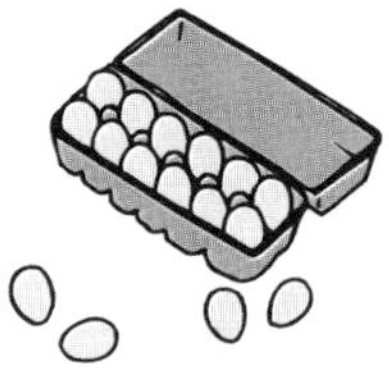

_____

100.00

Name: _____

Multiplication: Two-Digit Number x Two-Digit Number

Multiplication is a short way to find the sum of adding the same number a certain amount of times, such as 7 x 4 = 28 instead of 7 + 7 + 7 + 7 = 28.

Directions: Study the examples. Follow the steps to multiply by regrouping.

Example:

Step 1. Multiply by ones. Regroup.   Step 2. Multiply by tens. Regroup. Add.

```
  63            2                 1
  63            63                63              63
 x68           x8                x60             x68
  504          504               3780            504
+2780                                            3780
 4284                                            4284
```

```
  12            27                65              19
 x55           x15               x27             x39
```

```
  99            35                43              38
 x13           x14               x26             x17
 297           140
+990          +350
1287          4900
```

```
  53            47                57              48
 x86           x72               x62             x33
```

```
  27            93                64              53
 x54           x45               x16             x23
```

The Jones farm has 24 cows that each produce 52 quarts of milk a day.
How many quarts are produced each day altogether?   _____

Name: _____

Multiplication: Two-Digit Number x Three-Digit Number

Multiplication is a short way to find the sum of adding the same number a certain amount of times, such as 7 x 4 = 28 instead of 7 + 7 + 7 + 7 = 28.

Directions: Study the example. Follow the steps to multiply.

Example:

Step 1. Multiply by ones. Regroup. Step 2. Multiply by tens. Regroup. Add.

```
        2 2
287     287                          287        287
x43      x3                          x40        x43
        861                       11,480        861
                                            11,480
                                            12,341
```

```
261     434     357     614     368
x36     x48     x75     x59     x98
```

```
231     754     549     372     458
x46     x65     x89     x94     x85
```

At the Douglas berry farm, workers pick 378 baskets of strawberries each day. Each basket holds 65 strawberries. How many strawberries are picked each day?

_____

Name: _____

Multiplication: Three-Digit Number x Three-Digit Number

Multiplication is a short way to find the sum of adding the same number a certain amount of times, such as 7 x 4 = 28 instead of 7 + 7 + 7 + 7 = 28.

Directions: Multiply. Regroup when needed.

Example:

```
   563
  x248
  4504
 22520
112600
139,624
```

Hint: When multiplying by the tens, start writing the number in the tens place. When multiplying by the hundreds, start in the hundreds place.

842	932	759	531
x167	x272	x468	x556

383	523	229	738
x476	x349	x189	x513

483	946	365
x148	x367	x622

James grows pumpkins on his farm. He has 362 rows of pumpkins. There are 593 pumpkins in each row. How many pumpkins does James grow? _____

Name: _____

Multiplication

Multiplication is a short way to find the sum of adding the same number a certain amount of times, such as 7 x 4 = 28 instead of 7 + 7 + 7 + 7 = 28.

Directions: Multiply. Use your answers to follow the code to color the quilt.

70,725 — red	448 — white	34,088 — blue
667 — green	249,738 — orange	221,446 — yellow

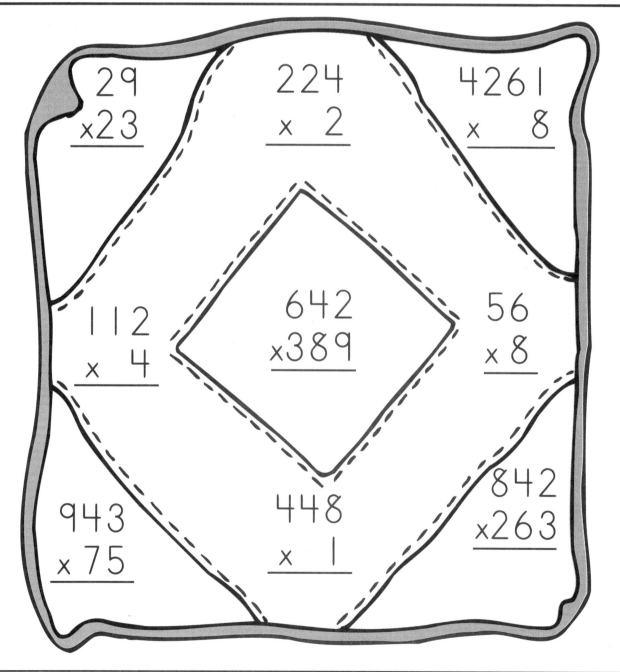

$$\begin{array}{r} 29 \\ \times 23 \\ \hline \end{array}$$

$$\begin{array}{r} 224 \\ \times\ \ 2 \\ \hline \end{array}$$

$$\begin{array}{r} 4261 \\ \times\ \ \ \ 8 \\ \hline \end{array}$$

$$\begin{array}{r} 112 \\ \times\ \ 4 \\ \hline \end{array}$$

$$\begin{array}{r} 642 \\ \times 389 \\ \hline \end{array}$$

$$\begin{array}{r} 56 \\ \times 8 \\ \hline \end{array}$$

$$\begin{array}{r} 943 \\ \times 75 \\ \hline \end{array}$$

$$\begin{array}{r} 448 \\ \times\ \ 1 \\ \hline \end{array}$$

$$\begin{array}{r} 842 \\ \times 263 \\ \hline \end{array}$$

Name: _____

Review

Directions: Multiply. Work the problem in the box. Color the ribbons blue if the answer is correct.

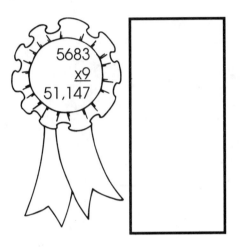

5683
x9
51,147

256
x38
8,728

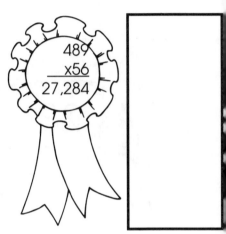

489
x56
27,284

356
x427
152,012

800
x7
6,300

60
x5
300

Name: _____

Division

Division is a way to find out how many times one number is contained in another number. For example, 28 ÷ 7 = 4 means that there are four groups of seven in 28.

Directions: Study the example. Then divide to solve the problems. Remember that the remainder must be smaller than the divisor.

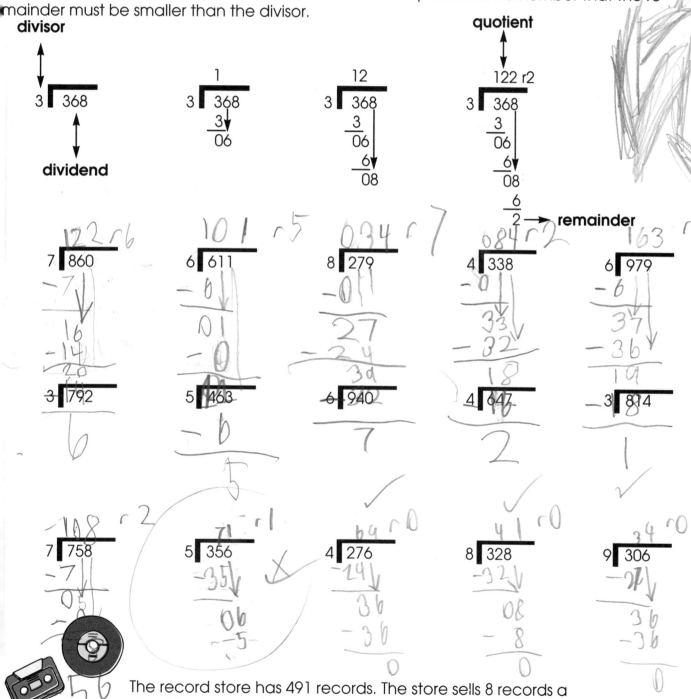

divisor

```
3 ) 368
```

dividend

```
  1
3 ) 368
    3
    06
```

```
 12
3 ) 368
    3
    06
    6
    08
```

quotient

```
 122 r2
3 ) 368
    3
    06
    6
    08
    6
    2  → remainder
```

```
122 r6
7 ) 860
  -7
   16
  -14
   20
```

```
101 r5
6 ) 611
  -0
   01
  -0
```

```
034 r7
8 ) 279
  -0
   27
  -24
   39
```

```
084 r2
4 ) 338
  -0
   33
  -32
   18
```

```
163 r1
6 ) 979
  -6
   37
  -36
   19
```

```
3 ) 792
```

```
5 ) 463
```

```
6 ) 940
   7
```

```
4 ) 647
   2
```

```
3 ) 814
   1
```

```
108 r2
7 ) 758
  -7
   05
```

```
71 r1
5 ) 356
  -35
   06
  -5
```

```
69 r0
4 ) 276
  -14
   36
  -36
   0
```

```
41 r0
8 ) 328
  -32
   08
  -8
   0
```

```
34 r0
9 ) 306
  -27
   36
  -36
   0
```

The record store has 491 records. The store sells 8 records a day. How many days will it take to sell all of the records? _____

Division: Checking The Answer

Division is a way to find out how many times one number is contained in another number. To check a division problem, multiply the quotient by the divisor. Add the remainder. The answer will be the dividend.

Directions: Study the example. Divide to work the problems. Draw a line from the division problem to the correct checking problem.

Example:

quotient

$$
\begin{array}{r}
58 \ r\,1 \\
\text{divisor} \rightarrow 3\overline{)175} \rightarrow \text{dividend} \\
\underline{15} \\
25 \\
\underline{24} \\
1 \rightarrow \text{remainder}
\end{array}
$$

Check:

$$
\begin{array}{r}
58 \leftarrow \text{quotient} \\
\underline{\times 3} \leftarrow \text{divisor} \\
174 \\
\underline{+1} \leftarrow \text{remainder} \\
175 \leftarrow \text{dividend}
\end{array}
$$

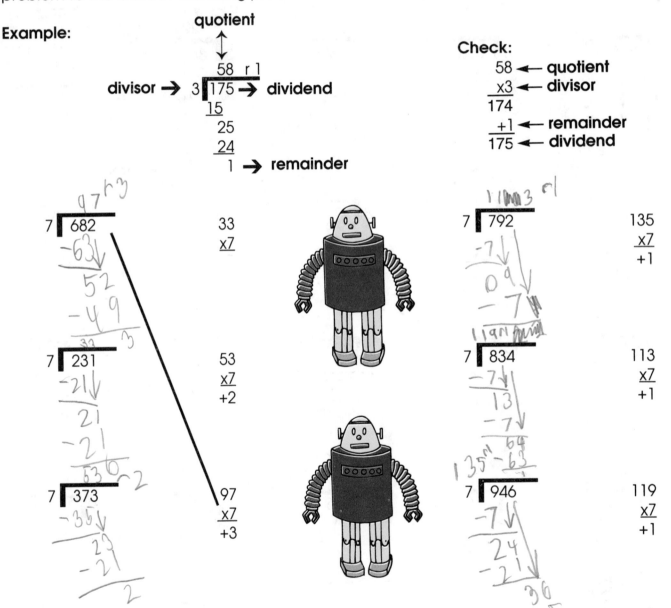

$7\overline{)682}$

33
x7

$7\overline{)792}$

135
x7
+1

$7\overline{)231}$

53
x7
+2

$7\overline{)834}$

113
x7
+1

$7\overline{)373}$

97
x7
+3

$7\overline{)946}$

119
x7
+1

The toy factory puts 7 robots in each box. The factory has 256 robots. How many boxes will they need? _____

Name: _____

Division: 1-Digit Divisor

Division is a way to find out how many times one number is contained in another number.

Directions: Work the problems on another sheet of paper. Use the code to color the picture.

Color these answers:

5)895	6)493	6)940	4)647	**orange**
4)672	6)696	5)749	8)628	**blue**
3)814	7)490	5)398	2)571	**black**

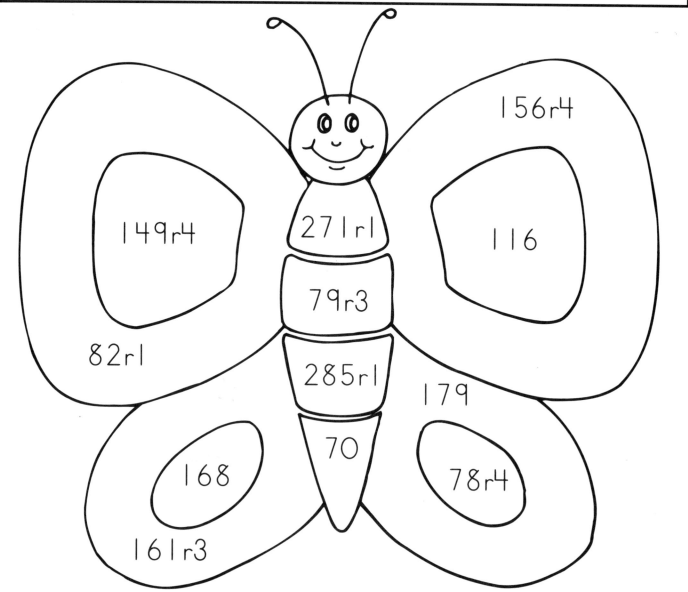

156r4

149r4

271r1

116

79r3

82r1

285r1

179

70

168

78r4

161r3

Name: _____

Division: 2-Digit Divisor

Division is a way to find out how many times one number is contained in another number.

Directions: Study the example. Divide. Remember to check your answer by multiplying it by the divisor and adding the remainder.

Example:

```
        2
  12 ) 256
       24
        1
```

```
        21 r4
  12 ) 256
       24
       16
       12
        4
```

Check: 21
        x12
         42
         21
        252
         +4
        256

27) 880   81) 913   65) 790   42) 674   67) 823

72) 977   54) 743   45) 863   24) 432   18) 372

28) 175   49) 538   77) 936   37) 603   63) 835

The Allen farm has 882 chickens. The chickens are kept in 21 coops.
How many chickens are there in each coop?   _____

Name: _____

Division: Checking The Answer

Division is a way to find out how many times one number is contained in another number.

Directions: Divide, then check your answers.

Example:

```
      182  r1          Check:      182
  4 ) 729                          x4
      4                            728
      32                           +1
      32                           729
       9
       8
       1
```

```
35 ) 468        check:  [        ]
                            x35
```

```
77 ) 819        check:  [        ]
                            x77
```

```
29 ) 568        check:  [        ]
                            x29
```

```
53 ) 2795       check:  [        ]
                            x53
```

```
67 ) 2856       check:  [        ]
                            x67
```

```
41 ) 6382       check:  [        ]
                            x41
```

The bookstore puts 53 books on a shelf. How many shelves will it need for 1590 books? _____

Name: _____

Averaging

An average is found by adding two or more quantities and then dividing by the number of quantities.

Directions: Study the example. Find the sum and divide by the number of quantities. Draw a line from each problem to the correct average.

Example:

$$24+36+30=90\div3$$
$$90 \div 3=30 \text{ Average}$$

$$\begin{array}{r} 30 \text{ Average} \\ 3\overline{)90} \\ \underline{9} \\ 00 \end{array}$$

12 + 14 + 29 + 1 =	410
4 + 10 + 25 =	83
33 +17 +14 + 20 + 16 =	40
782 + 276 + 172 =	15
81 + 82 + 91 + 78 =	13
21 + 34 + 44 =	33
14 + 24 + 10 + 31 + 5 + 6 =	14
278 + 246 =	20
48 + 32 + 18 + 62 =	262

A baseball player had 3 hits in game 1, 2 hits in game 2, and 4 hits in game 3. How many hits did she average over the three games? _____

Name: _____

Averaging

An average is found by adding two or more quantities and then dividing by the number of quantities.

Directions: Find the averages.

Ted went bowling. He had scores of 112, 124, and 100. What was his average?

_____

Sue ran three races. Her times were 9 seconds, 10 seconds, and 8 seconds. What was her average?

_____

The baseball team played six games. They had 12 hits, 6 hits 18 hits, 36 hits, 11 hits, and 7 hits. What is the average number of hits in a game?

_____

n three games of football, Chris gained 156, 268, and 176 yards running. How many yards did he average in a game?

_____

Jane scored 18,15, 26, and 21 points in four basketball games. How many points did she average?

_____

Name: _____

Review

Directions: Divide.

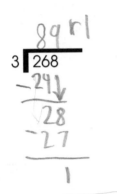

$$\begin{array}{r} 89\ r1 \\ 3\overline{\smash{)}268} \\ -24\downarrow \\ \hline 28 \\ -27 \\ \hline 1 \end{array}$$

$$\begin{array}{r} 11\ r0 \\ 15\overline{\smash{)}165} \\ -15\downarrow \\ \hline 15 \\ -15 \\ \hline 0 \end{array}$$

27 ⟌ 489   48 ⟌ 695

79 ⟌ 937   49 ⟌ 683   91 ⟌ 848   73 ⟌ 592   59 ⟌ 473

23 ⟌ 1268   67 ⟌ 2543   81 ⟌ 3608   37 ⟌ 8432   97 ⟌ 4528

Directions: Find the averages. An average is found by adding two or more quantities and then dividing by the number of quantities.

22, 38 _____   105, 263, 331 _____

48, 100, 62 _____   248, 325, 250, 69 _____

17, 18, 36, 28, 6 _____   87, 91, 55, 48, 119 _____

26

Name: _____

Fraction: Addition

A fraction is a number that names part of a whole, such as 1/2 or 1/3. The denominator is the bottom number in a fraction; the numerator is the top number.

When adding fractions with the same denominator, the denominator stays the same. Add only the numerators.

Example:

numerator → $\dfrac{1}{8}$ + $\dfrac{2}{8}$ = $\dfrac{3}{8}$
denominator →

Directions: Study the example. Add the fractions. The first one is done for you.

$$\dfrac{3}{4} \quad \dfrac{2}{4} \quad \dfrac{1}{4}$$

$$\dfrac{3}{4} \quad \dfrac{1}{4} \quad 1$$

$$\dfrac{1}{4} \quad \dfrac{1}{2}$$

$$\dfrac{1}{3} \quad \dfrac{2}{9} \quad \dfrac{3}{9} \quad \dfrac{4}{9} \quad \dfrac{6}{9} \quad \dfrac{7}{9}$$

$$\dfrac{4}{9} \quad \dfrac{1}{9} \quad \dfrac{5}{9} \quad \dfrac{2}{3}$$

$$\dfrac{5}{9} \quad \dfrac{7}{9} \quad \dfrac{8}{9}$$

$$\dfrac{4}{5} \quad \dfrac{2}{5} \quad \dfrac{2}{5} \quad \dfrac{3}{5} \quad \dfrac{1}{5}$$

$$\dfrac{3}{5} \quad 1$$

27

Name: _____

Fractions: Subtraction

A fraction is a number that names part of a whole, such as 1/2 or 1/3. The denominator is the bottom number in a fraction; the numerator is the top number.

When subtracting fractions with the same denominator, the denominator stays the same. Subtract only the numerators.

Directions: Solve the problems below, working from left to right across each row. As you find each answer, copy the letter from the code box into the numbered blanks. The first one is done for you. The answer will tell the name of a famous American.

1. $\dfrac{3}{8} - \dfrac{2}{8} = \underline{\dfrac{1}{8}}$ 2. $\dfrac{2}{4} - \dfrac{1}{4} = \underline{\dfrac{1}{4}}$ 3. $\dfrac{5}{9} - \dfrac{3}{9} = \underline{\dfrac{2}{9}}$ 4. $\dfrac{2}{3} - \dfrac{1}{3} = \underline{\dfrac{1}{3}}$

5. $\dfrac{8}{12} - \dfrac{7}{12} = \underline{\dfrac{1}{12}}$ 6. $\dfrac{4}{5} - \dfrac{1}{5} = \underline{\dfrac{3}{5}}$ 7. $\dfrac{6}{12} - \dfrac{3}{12} = \underline{\dfrac{1}{4}}$ 8. $\dfrac{4}{9} - \dfrac{1}{9} = \underline{\dfrac{1}{3}}$

9. $\dfrac{11}{12} - \dfrac{7}{12} = \underline{\dfrac{4}{12}}$ 10. $\dfrac{7}{8} - \dfrac{3}{8} = \underline{\dfrac{1}{2}}$ 11. $\dfrac{4}{7} - \dfrac{2}{7} = \underline{\dfrac{2}{7}}$ 12. $\dfrac{14}{16} - \dfrac{7}{16} = \underline{\dfrac{7}{16}}$

13. $\dfrac{18}{20} - \dfrac{13}{20} = \underline{\dfrac{1}{4}}$ 14. $\dfrac{13}{15} - \dfrac{2}{15} = \underline{\dfrac{11}{15}}$ 15. $\dfrac{5}{6} - \dfrac{3}{6} = \underline{\dfrac{1}{3}}$

Code Box				
T 1/8	p 5/24	h 1/4	f 4/12	e 2/7
J 3/12	e 3/9	o 2/9	f 4/8	r 7/16
o 2/8	y 8/20	q 1/32	m 1/3	s 5/20
a 1/12	r 12/15	s 3/5	n 2/6	o 11/15

Who helped write the Declaration of Independence?

1. $\underline{T}$ 2. $\underline{H}$ 3. $\underline{O}$ 4. $\underline{M}$ 5. $\underline{A}$ 6. $\underline{S}$

7. $\underline{J}$ 8. $\underline{E}$ 9. $\underline{F}$ 10. $\underline{F}$ 11. $\underline{E}$ 12. $\underline{R}$ 13. $\underline{S}$ 14. $\underline{O}$ 15. $\underline{N}$

Name: _____

Fractions: Adding Mixed Numerals

A mixed numeral is a number written as a whole number and a fraction, such as 6 5/8.

Directions: Add the number in the center to the numbers in the rings.

Example:

$$9 \frac{1}{3}$$
$$+3 \frac{1}{3}$$
$$12 \frac{2}{3}$$

$$2 \frac{3}{6}$$
$$+1 \frac{1}{6}$$
$$3 \frac{4}{6}$$

$9\frac{1}{3} + 3\frac{1}{3}$

$12\frac{2}{3}$

$12\frac{4}{3}$

$13\frac{1}{3}$

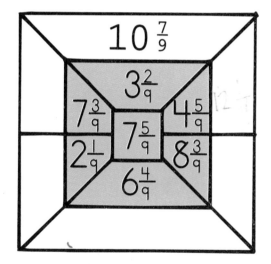

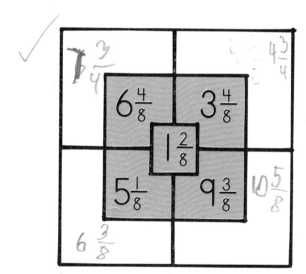

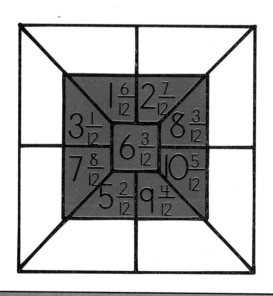

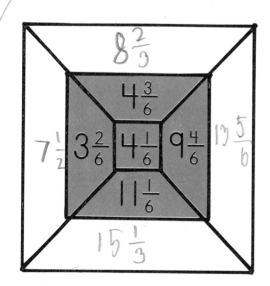

Name: _____

Fractions: Subtracting Mixed Numerals

A mixed numeral is a number written as a whole number and a fraction, such as 6 5/8.

Directions: Solve the problems. The first one is done for you.

$7\frac{3}{8}$ $-4\frac{2}{8}$ $= 3\frac{1}{8}$

$4\frac{5}{6}$ $-3\frac{1}{6}$

$4\frac{1}{2}$ -3

$7\frac{5}{8}$ $-6\frac{3}{8}$

$6\frac{6}{8}$ $-1\frac{1}{8}$

$5\frac{3}{4}$ $-1\frac{1}{4}$

$5\frac{2}{3}$ $-3\frac{1}{3}$

$4\frac{8}{10}$ $-3\frac{3}{10}$

$9\frac{8}{9}$ $-4\frac{3}{9}$

$7\frac{2}{3}$ $-6\frac{1}{3}$

$7\frac{2}{3}$ -5

$9\frac{8}{10}$ $-6\frac{3}{10}$

$4\frac{7}{9}$ -2

$6\frac{7}{8}$ $-5\frac{3}{8}$

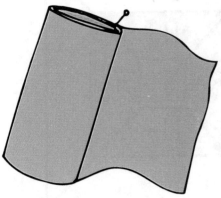

$6\frac{3}{4}$ $-3\frac{1}{4}$

$5\frac{6}{7}$ $-3\frac{1}{7}$

$7\frac{6}{7}$ $-2\frac{4}{7}$

Sally needs 1 3/8 yards of cloth to make a dress. She has 4 5/8 yards. How much will be left over?

_____

Name: _____

Fractions: Equivalent

Equivalent fractions name the same number, such as 1/2 and 2/4.

Directions: Study the example. Draw a line between the equivalent fractions in each row.

Example:

Equivalent fractions are equal to each other.

$$1/2 = 2/4 = 4/8$$

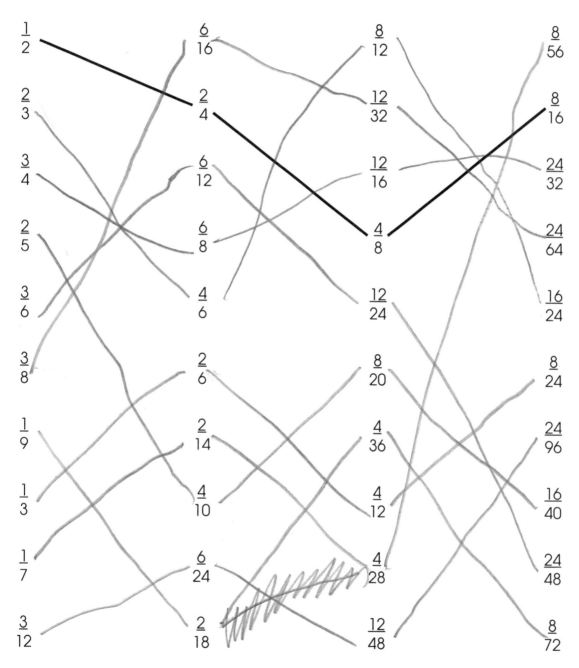

$\frac{1}{2}$ $\frac{6}{16}$ $\frac{8}{12}$ $\frac{8}{56}$

$\frac{2}{3}$ $\frac{2}{4}$ $\frac{12}{32}$ $\frac{8}{16}$

$\frac{3}{4}$ $\frac{6}{12}$ $\frac{12}{16}$ $\frac{24}{32}$

$\frac{2}{5}$ $\frac{6}{8}$ $\frac{4}{8}$ $\frac{24}{64}$

$\frac{3}{6}$ $\frac{4}{6}$ $\frac{12}{24}$ $\frac{16}{24}$

$\frac{3}{8}$ $\frac{2}{6}$ $\frac{8}{20}$ $\frac{8}{24}$

$\frac{1}{9}$ $\frac{2}{14}$ $\frac{4}{36}$ $\frac{24}{96}$

$\frac{1}{3}$ $\frac{4}{10}$ $\frac{4}{12}$ $\frac{16}{40}$

$\frac{1}{7}$ $\frac{6}{24}$ $\frac{4}{28}$ $\frac{24}{48}$

$\frac{3}{12}$ $\frac{2}{18}$ $\frac{12}{48}$ $\frac{8}{72}$

31

Name: _____

Fractions: Reducing

Reducing a fraction means to find the greatest common factor and divide.

Directions: Reduce each fraction. Circle the answer.

Example: $\frac{5}{15} = \frac{1}{3}$ factors of 5:   1, 5 $5 \div 5 = 1$

factors of 15:   1, 3, 5, 15 $15 \div 5 = 3$

$\frac{2}{4} = $ $\frac{1}{2}, \frac{1}{6}, \frac{1}{8}$ $\frac{3}{9} = $ $\frac{1}{6}, \frac{1}{3}, \frac{3}{6}$ $\frac{5}{10} = $ $\frac{1}{5}, \frac{1}{2}, \frac{5}{6}$

$\frac{4}{12} = $ $\frac{1}{4}, \frac{1}{3}, \frac{2}{3}$ $\frac{10}{15} = $ $\frac{2}{3}, \frac{2}{5}, \frac{2}{7}$ $\frac{12}{14} = $ $\frac{1}{8}, \frac{6}{7}, \frac{3}{5}$

$\frac{3}{24} = $ $\frac{2}{12}, \frac{3}{6}, \frac{1}{8}$ $\frac{1}{11} = $ $\frac{1}{11}, \frac{2}{5}, \frac{3}{4}$ $\frac{11}{22} = $ $\frac{1}{12}, \frac{1}{2}, \frac{2}{5}$

Directions: Find the way home. Color the boxes with fractions equivalent to 1/8 and 1/3.

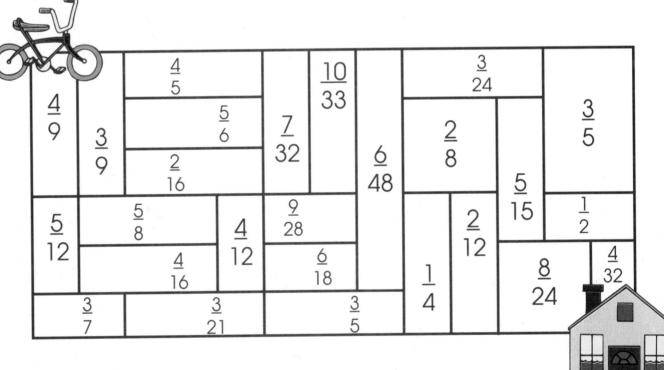

Name: _____

Fractions: Mixed Numerals

A mixed numeral is a number written as a whole number and a fraction, such as 6 5/8.

Directions: Change each fraction to a mixed numeral. Make the mixed numerals into fractions.

Example:

To change a fraction into a mixed numeral, divide the denominator (bottom number) into the numerator (top number). Put the remainder over the denominator.

To change a mixed numeral into a fraction, multiply the denominator by the whole number, add the numerator, and place it on top of the denominator.

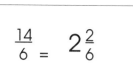

$$\frac{14}{6} = 2\frac{2}{6} \qquad 6\overline{)14} \begin{array}{c} 2\ r2 \\ \underline{12} \\ 2 \end{array}$$

$$3\frac{1}{7} = \frac{22}{7} \qquad (7 \times 3) + 1 = \frac{22}{7}$$

$$\frac{21}{6} = \text{\_\_\_\_}$$

$$4\frac{3}{8} = \frac{\boxed{}}{8}$$

$$\frac{11}{8} = \text{\_\_\_\_}$$

$$\frac{24}{5} = \text{\_\_\_\_}$$

$$2\frac{1}{3} = \frac{\boxed{}}{3}$$

$$\frac{21}{4} = \text{\_\_\_\_}$$

$$\frac{10}{3} = \text{\_\_\_\_}$$

$$4\frac{3}{5} = \frac{\boxed{}}{5}$$

$$\frac{33}{5} = \text{\_\_\_\_}$$

$$\frac{21}{4} = \text{\_\_\_\_}$$

$$3\frac{4}{6} = \frac{\boxed{}}{6}$$

$$\frac{13}{6} = \text{\_\_\_\_}$$

$$\frac{11}{6} = \text{\_\_\_\_}$$

$$7\frac{1}{4} = \frac{\boxed{}}{4}$$

$$\frac{23}{7} = \text{\_\_\_\_}$$

$$\frac{13}{4} = \text{\_\_\_\_}$$

$$2\frac{3}{5} = \frac{\boxed{}}{5}$$

$$8\frac{1}{3} = \text{\_\_\_\_}$$

$$\frac{12}{5} = \text{\_\_\_\_}$$

$$7\frac{1}{2} = \frac{\boxed{}}{2}$$

$$9\frac{3}{7} = \text{\_\_\_\_}$$

$$\frac{10}{9} = \text{\_\_\_\_}$$

$$6\frac{5}{7} = \frac{\boxed{}}{7}$$

$$\frac{32}{24} = \text{\_\_\_\_}$$

Name: _____

Review

Directions: Add or subtract the fractions and mixed numerals.

$\frac{3}{8} - \frac{1}{8} =$ ___ $\frac{3}{4} - \frac{2}{4} =$ ___ $\frac{3}{5} + \frac{1}{5} =$ ___ $\frac{4}{12} + \frac{3}{12} =$ ___ $\frac{3}{9} + \frac{1}{9} =$ ___

$$3 \ \frac{1}{8}$$
$$+1 \ \frac{3}{8}$$

$$4 \ \frac{5}{6}$$
$$-3 \ \frac{1}{6}$$

$$7 \ \frac{5}{11}$$
$$+3 \ \frac{3}{11}$$

$$8 \ \frac{3}{9}$$
$$+2 \ \frac{5}{9}$$

$$4 \ \frac{7}{8}$$
$$-2 \ \frac{5}{8}$$

Directions: Reduce the fractions. Circle the answers.

$\frac{3}{6} =$	$\frac{1}{7}$ $\frac{1}{2}$ $\frac{1}{4}$	$\frac{2}{8} =$	$\frac{1}{3}$ $\frac{1}{4}$ $\frac{1}{16}$	$\frac{4}{6} =$	$\frac{1}{4}$ $\frac{2}{3}$ $\frac{3}{9}$
$\frac{4}{20} =$	$\frac{1}{4}$ $\frac{1}{3}$ $\frac{1}{5}$	$\frac{7}{21} =$	$\frac{1}{7}$ $\frac{1}{3}$ $\frac{1}{5}$	$\frac{9}{12} =$	$\frac{3}{5}$ $\frac{1}{8}$ $\frac{3}{4}$

Directions: Reduce the fractions.

$\frac{6}{24} =$ _____ $\frac{8}{32} =$ _____ $\frac{2}{4} =$ _____

$\frac{3}{15} =$ _____ $\frac{6}{12} =$ _____ $\frac{3}{9} =$ _____

Directions: Change the mixed numerals to fractions and the fractions to mixed numerals.

$3 \ \frac{1}{3} = \frac{\square}{3}$ $\frac{14}{4} =$ _____ $\frac{26}{6} =$ _____ $3 \ \frac{7}{12} = \frac{\square}{12}$ $\frac{22}{7} =$ _____

Name: _____

Decimals

A decimal is a number with one or more places to the right of a decimal point, such as 5.5 or 2.25. A decimal point is the dot between the ones place and the tenths place.

Directions: Add or subtract. Remember to include the decimal point in your answer.

Example:

1 3/10 = 1.3   1 6/10 = 1.6

$$
\begin{array}{r} 1.3 \\ +1.6 \\ \hline 2.9 \end{array}
$$

8.1 +1.7	4.1 +6.2	0.5 +1.6	7.6 -6.5	7.2 -2.6	1.2 +5.0
8.7 -3.9	6.8 -3.7	7.8 -6.8	16.5 -7.3	6.4 +5.3	10.0 +3.5
.42 +.35	.98 -.87	.78 -.13	.83 +.12	.95 -.14	3.23 +2.48
4.68 -2.65	5.86 -2.73	6.98 +1.40	3.27 +1.82	4.65 -1.32	5.97 +2.77

Mr. Martin went on a car trip with his family. Mr. Martin purchased gas three times. He bought 6.7 gallons, 7.3 gallons, then 5.8 gallons of gas. How much gas did he purchase in all?

_____

35

Name: _____

Decimals

A decimal is a number with one or more places to the right of a decimal point, such as 6.5 or 2.25.

Directions: Fill in the circle next to the correct answer.

Example:

1.7	○ 2.5
+2.4	○ 3.1
	● 4.1

2.8	○ 5.2	5.7	○ 1.9	7.6	○ 15.9
+3.4	○ 7.4	-3.8	○ 2.5	+8.9	○ 16.5
	○ 6.2		○ 2.9		○ 17.3

16.3	○ 25.11	28.6	○ 73.6	43.9	○ 100.4
+9.8	○ 26.1	+43.9	○ 72.5	+56.5	○ 107.4
	○ 26.01		○ 71.9		○ 101.4

12.87	○ 16.32	47.56	○ 13.61	93.6	○ 14.8
-3.45	○ 10.31	-33.95	○ 80.41	-79.8	○ 15.3
	○ 9.42		○ 14.61		○ 13.8

11.57	○ 22.21	27.83	○ 14.09	106.935	○ 111.1
+10.64	○ 1.93	-14.94	○ 12.89	-95.824	○ 111.11
	○ 21.12		○ 11.97		○ 11.111

The high-speed train traveled 87.90 miles day one, 127.86 miles on day two, and 113.41 miles on day three. How many miles did it travel in all?

_____

36

Decimals

A decimal is a number with one or more places to the right of a decimal point, such as 6.5 or 2.25. A fraction is a number that names part of a whole, such as 1/2 or 1/3.

Directions: Compare the fraction in each box to the decimal. Circle the larger number. Use this picture to help.

Example:

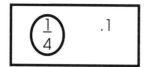

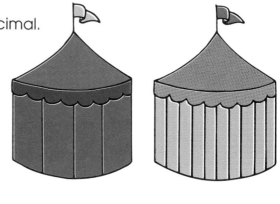

fourths   tenths

$\frac{2}{4}$ .2	$\frac{3}{4}$ .3	.6 $\frac{1}{2}$	$\frac{1}{4}$ .4	$\frac{1}{3}$ .1
$\frac{1}{4}$ .7	.8 $\frac{2}{4}$	$\frac{3}{4}$ .9	$\frac{5}{6}$ .5	.6 $\frac{2}{5}$
$\frac{3}{12}$ .9	$\frac{1}{6}$ .2	$\frac{2}{3}$ .8	.3 $\frac{1}{5}$	.7 $\frac{2}{5}$
$\frac{3}{10}$ .5	$\frac{1}{9}$ .4	$\frac{4}{5}$ .7	.7 $\frac{1}{3}$	.1 $\frac{6}{12}$

Name: _____

Identifying Operations

Directions: Write the correct sign for each worked problem in each circle. The first one is done for you.

   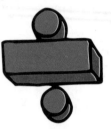

5 (**X**) 6 = 30	.3 ( ) .2 = .1	128 ( ) 56 = 72
4 ( ) 8 = 32	$1\frac{5}{6}$ ( ) $2\frac{2}{6}$ = $4\frac{1}{6}$	49 ( ) 7 = 7
54 ( ) 6 = 9	1/10 ( ) 2/5 = 5/10	188 ( ) 21 = 209
38 ( ) 7 = 31	5 ( ) 7 = 35	5 ( ) 3 = 15
28 ( ) 16 = 44	$3\frac{3}{8}$ ( ) $2\frac{1}{4}$ = $1\frac{1}{8}$	16 ( ) 4 = 4
32 ( ) 8 = 4	9 ( ) 3 = 6	47 ( ) 38 = 9
63 ( ) 7 = 9	12 ( ) 12 = 144	10 ( ) 0 = 0
49 ( ) 9 = 40	100 ( ) 5 = 20	.91 ( ) .81 = .1
48 ( ) 12 = 4	98 ( ) 43 = 55	3/10 ( ) .3 = .6
39 ( ) 19 = 20	.9 ( ) .7 = .2	.5 ( ) 1/2 = 1.0
72 ( ) 8 = 9	1.68 ( ) .9 = .78	.97 ( ) 5/10 = 1.47

Name: _____

Operations

Directions: Solve the problems. Circle the letter with the correct answer. Write the letters in order to read the message.

1.	348 - 227	121	M	425	S
2.	542 x 6	5683	W	3252	A
3.	328 + 593	921	T	149	N
4.	1280 ÷ 40	92	L	32	H
5.	24 x 52	2386	W	1248	I
6.	863 - 438	425	S	234	U
7.	4586 + 1097	3489	Q	5683	W
8.	480 ÷ 4	32	H	120	O
9.	.5 + .9	1.4	N	.14	E
10.	1.6 - .9	.7	D	.9	T
11.	$3\frac{1}{4} + 2\frac{1}{5}$	$5\frac{9}{20}$	E	$4\frac{7}{20}$	L
12.	4/8 -1/4	3/8	Y	1/4	R
13.	2193 -1864	329	F	591	Y
14.	26 x 9	234	U	744	L
15.	42 ÷ 6	8	M	7	L

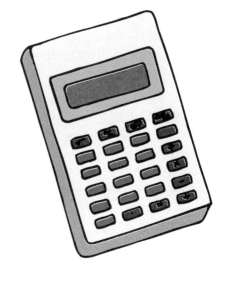

1. _____ 2. _____ 3. _____ 4. _____ 5. _____ 6. _____

7. _____ 8. _____ 9. _____ 10. _____ 11. _____ 12. _____ 13. _____ 14. _____ 15. _____ !

39

Name: _____

Estimating

It is not always necessary to find an exact number. In such cases, we can estimate the answer. To estimate means to give an approximate rather than an exact answer. To do this, round up numbers over 50 to the nearest hundred. Example: 251 is rounded up to 300. Round down numbers less than 50 to the next lowest hundred. Example: 128 is rounded down to 100.

Directions: Round the numbers, then work the problems.
The first one is done for you.

Example:

Problem:
Jack and Alex were playing a computer game. Jack scored 428 points. Alex scored 132. About how many more points did Jack score than Alex?

Answer:
Round Jack's 428 points down to the nearest hundred, 400.   400
Round Alex's 132 points down to 100. Subtract.   -100
                                        estimate   300

Jack scored about 300 points more than Alex.

258 → 300 +117 → 100 400	493 → +114 →	837 → -252 →
928 → -437 →	700 → -491 →	319 → +630 →
332 → +567 →	493 → -162 →	1356 → +2941 →

Name: _____

Estimating

To estimate means to give an approximate rather than an exact answer. Estimating can help us in many ways. One way is planning time.

Directions: Follow the steps to estimate the time it will take to read a book.

Step 1: Write down the number of pages in the book you want to read.

<u>148</u> pages

Step 2: Pick a page that is of average length. Time yourself to see how long it takes you to read the page.

_____

Step 3: Suppose it took you 4 minutes to read the page. How many minutes will it take to read the book?

_____

Step 4: Estimate the number of hours it will take to read the book by rounding 592 minutes up to 600 minutes.

_____

Name: _____

Review

Directions: Add or subtract to find the answer.

Jake's times for the 100-meter dash were 10.1 seconds, 12.5 seconds, and 11.8 seconds. What was his total time?

_____

Bill jumped 28.5 feet. Jim jumped 27.3 feet. How much farther did Bill jump than Jim?

_____

Sue threw the discus 86.4 feet. Julie threw the discus 93.8 feet. How much farther did Julie throw the discus than Sue?

_____

Kim, Monica, and Kelly swam on the same team in the butterfly relay race. Their individual scores were 32.8 seconds, 29.9 seconds, and 31.7 seconds. The winning team's time was 93.5 seconds. Did Kim, Monica, and Kelly swim the fastest race?

_____

Directions: Decide which sign is correct for each problem: +, -, x, or ÷. Write it in the circle.

5 ◯ 5 = 25   100 ◯ 25 = 4   42 ◯ 38 = 80

152 ◯ 38 = 114   72 ◯ 12 = 6   9 ◯ 5 = 45

Directions: Round the numbers, then estimate each answer.

$$592 \rightarrow$$
$$+312 \rightarrow$$

$$802 \rightarrow$$
$$-695 \rightarrow$$

$$449 \rightarrow$$
$$-299 \rightarrow$$

$$612 \rightarrow$$
$$+499 \rightarrow$$

Name: _____

Measurement: Inches

An inch is a measurement of length in the customary system. It is this long: _____ .

Directions: Use a ruler to measure each foot to the nearest inch.

_____

_____

_____

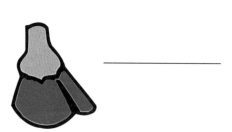

_____

_____

_____

_____

Measurement: Fractions Of An Inch

An inch is a measurement of length in the customary system. It is this long: _____

Directions: Use a ruler to measure to the nearest quarter of an inch.

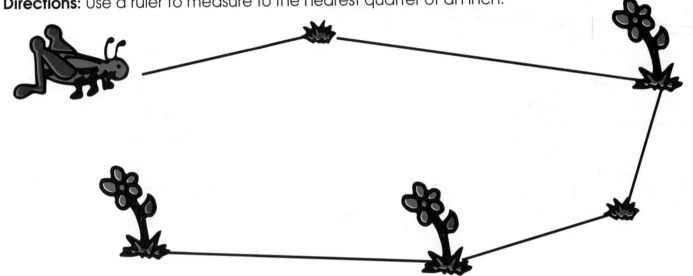

How far did the grasshopper jump?   _____ + _____ + _____ + _____ + _____ = _____

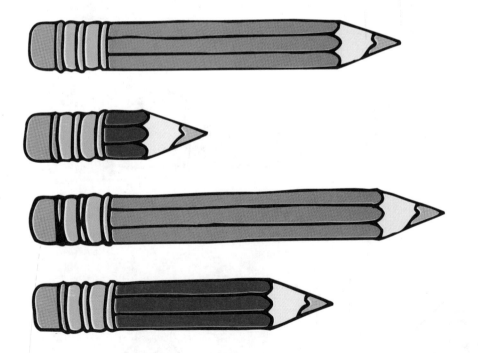

What is the total length of the pencils?   _____ + _____ + _____ + _____ = _____

Name: _____

Measurement: Foot, Yard, Mile

Directions: Choose the measure of distance you would use for each object.

1 foot = 12 inches
1 yard = 3 feet
1 mile = 1760 yards

 ___inches___

 _____

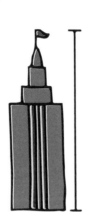 _____

 _____

 _____

 _____

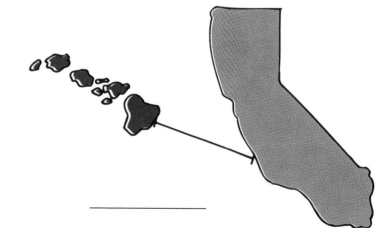 _____

45

Name: _____

Measurement: Perimeter And Area

The perimeter is the distance around a figure. The perimeter is found by adding the lengths of the sides.

The area is the number of square units needed to cover a region. The area is found by adding the number of square units. A unit can be any unit of measure. Most often inches, feet, or yards are used.

Directions: Find the perimeter and area for each figure. The first one is done for you.

☐ =1 square unit

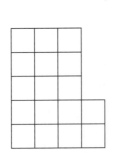

Perimeter = __18__ units

Area = __17__ sq. units

Perimeter = _____ units

Area = _____ sq. units

Perimeter = _____ units

Area = _____ sq. units

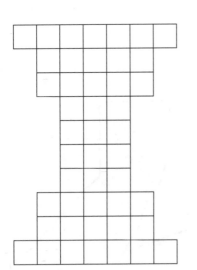

Perimeter = _____ units

Area = _____ sq. units

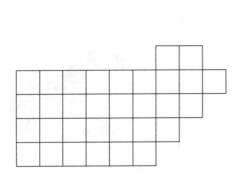

Perimeter = _____ units

Area = _____ sq. units

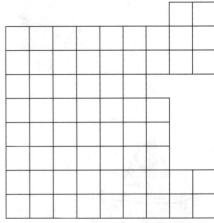

Perimeter = _____ units

Area = _____ sq. units

Name: _____

Volume

Volume is the number of cubic units that fit inside a figure.

Directions: Find the volume of each figure. The first one is done for you.

__4__ cubic units

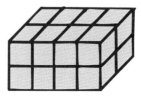

_____ cubic units

_____ cubic units

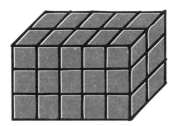

_____ cubic units

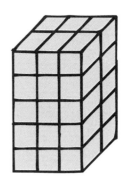

_____ cubic units

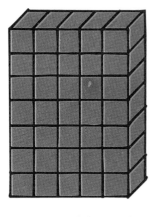

_____ cubic units

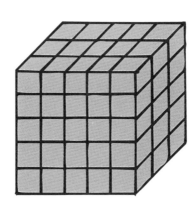

_____ cubic units

_____ cubic units

Name: _____

Measurement: Ounce, Pound, Ton

Directions: Decide whether to use ounces, pounds, or tons to weigh each of the following.

ounce

pound

ton

16 ounces = 1 pound
2000 pounds = 1 ton

ounces _____

_____

_____

_____

_____

_____

_____

_____

Measurement: Cup, Pint, Quart, Gallon

The cup, pint, quart, and gallon are units in the customary system for measuring liquids.

Directions: Circle the number of objects on the right side of the problem that equal the same amount as the objects on the left. The first one is done for you.

2 cups = 1 pint
2 pints = 1 quart
4 quarts = 1 gallon

 =1 cup   =1 pint  = 1 quart  = 1 gallon

 =   =

    =

 =

    =

Name: _____

Review

Directions: Find the perimeter and area. The perimeter is found by adding the lengths of the sides. The area is found by adding the number of square units.

 = 1 sq. unit

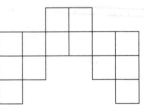

Perimeter = _____ units
Area = _____ sq. units

Perimeter = _____ units
Area = _____ sq. units

Directions: How much does it equal?

= _____ pints

= _____ quarts

Directions: Write whether you would use ounce, pound, or ton to weigh each of the following.

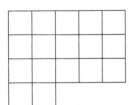

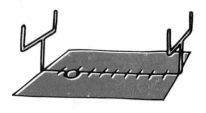

_____   _____   _____

Directions: Write whether you would use inch, foot, yard, or mile to measure the following.

_____   _____   _____

Name: _____

Measurement: Centimeters

A centimeter is a measurement of length in the metric system. You can write **cm.** for centimeter.

Directions: Use a centimeter ruler to measure the foot of each animal to the nearest centimeter.

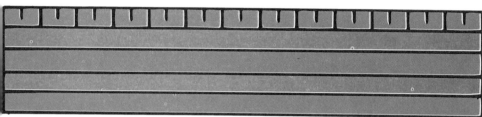

_____

_____

_____

_____

_____

_____

51

Name: _____

Measurement: Meters And Kilometers

Meters and kilometers are distance measurements in the metric system. A meter is equal to 100 centimeters. It is a little longer than a yard — 39.37 inches (a yard is 36 inches). A door-knob is about 1 meter from the floor. You can write **m** to stand for meter.

Kilometers are used to measure long distances, such as the distance traveled by a car. There are 1000 meters in a kilometer. A kilometer is equal to about 5/8 of a mile. You can write **km** to stand for kilometer.

Directions: Choose the measure of distance you would use for each object.

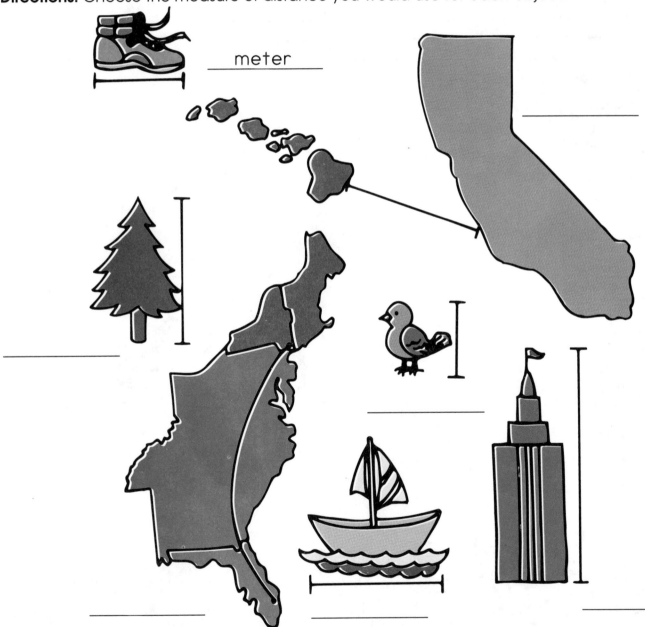

meter

Name: _____

Measurement: Perimeter, Area, And Volume

The perimeter is the distance around a figure. The area is the number of square units needed to cover a region.

Directions: Find the perimeter and area of each figure.

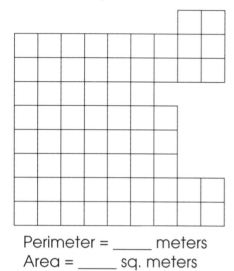

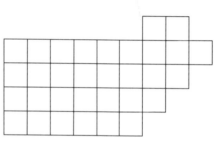

☐ = 1 sq. meter

Perimeter = _____ meters
Area = _____ sq. meters

Perimeter = _____ meters
Area = _____ sq. meters

Directions: The volume is the number of cubic units that fit inside a figure. Find the volume of each figure.

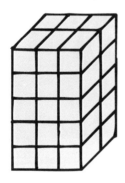

_____ cubic meters

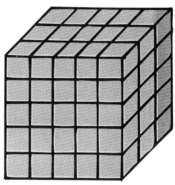

_____ cubic meters

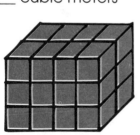

_____ cubic meters

_____ cubic meters

53

Name: _____

Measurement: Gram And Kilogram

Grams and kilograms are measurements of weight in the metric system. A gram weighs about 1/28 of an ounce. There are 1000 grams in a kilogram. A Kilogram weighs about 2.2 pounds.

Directions: Decide whether to use grams or kilograms to measure each of the following.

grams

Name: _____

Measurements: Milliliter And Liter

Liters and milliliters are units in the metric system for measuring liquids.
A milliliter (**mL** stands for milliliter) equals .001 liter.
Liters (**L**) measure large amounts of liquid. There are 1000 milliliters in a liter.

Directions: Choose milliliters or liters to measure these liquids.

millileter

_____

_____   _____

_____   _____

_____   _____

Temperature: Celsius

Temperature tells us how hot or cold something is. The degree Celsius is used to measure temperature in the metric system. °C stands for degree Celsius.

0° C

30° C

Directions: Use the thermometer to answer the questions.

At what temperature does
water boil? _____

At what temperature does
water freeze? _____

What is the normal body
temperature? _____

Is it a hot or cold day when
the temperature is 42° C? _____

Is it a hot or cold day when
the temperature is 5° C? _____

What temperature best describes a hot summer day?

　5° C　　40° C　　20° C

What temperature best describes an icy winter day?

　0° C　　15° C　　10° C

Name: _____

Temperature: Fahrenheit

The degree Fahrenheit is used to measure temperature in the customary system. °F stands for degree Fahrenheit.

28° F

72° F

Directions: Use the thermometer to answer these questions.

At what temperature does water boil?   _____

At what temperature does water freeze?   _____

What is the normal body temperature?   _____

Is a 100° F day warm, hot, or cold?   _____

Is a 0° F day warm, hot, or cold?   _____

Which temperature best describes room temperature?

   58° F   70° F   80° F

Which temperature best describes a cold winter day?

   22° F   38° F   32° F

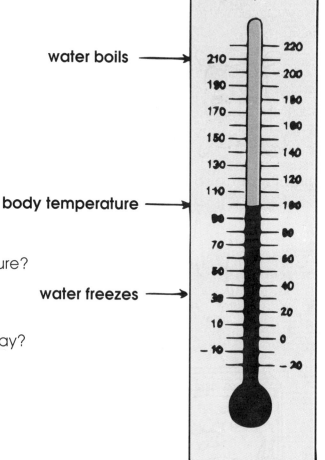

water boils →

body temperature →

water freezes →

Review

Directions: Choose centimeter, meter, or kilometer to measure each of the following.

the height of a tree _____

height of a building _____

length of a shoe _____

length of the school yard _____

distance around the earth _____

distance a plane flies _____

Directions: Choose grams or kilograms to measure each of the following.

 _____

 _____

 _____

 _____

Directions: Choose liters or milliliters to measure each of the following.

 _____

 _____

 _____

Name: _____

Graphs

A graph is a drawing that shows information about changes in numbers.

Directions: Answer the questions by reading the graphs.

Bar Graph

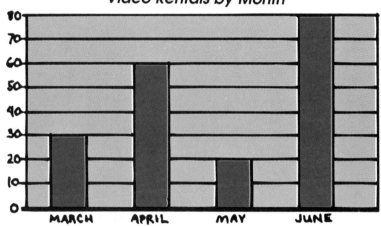

Video Rentals by Month

How many videos did the store rent in June? _____

What month did the store rent the fewest videos? _____

How many videos did the store rent for all four months? _____

Line Graph

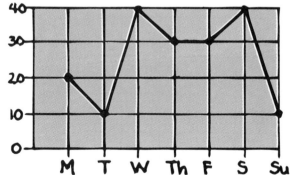

Records Sold by Days of Week

On which day did the store sell the fewest records? _____

How many records did the store sell in one week? _____

Name: _____

Ordered Pairs

An ordered pair is a pair of numbers used to locate a point.

Example: (8, 3)
Step 1: Count across to line 8 on the graph.
Step 2: Count up to line 3 on the graph.
Step 3: Draw a dot to mark the spot.

Directions: Map the following spots on the grid using ordered pairs.

(4, 7)	(2, 2)
(9, 10)	(1, 5)
(2, 1)	(7, 4)
(5, 6)	(3, 8)

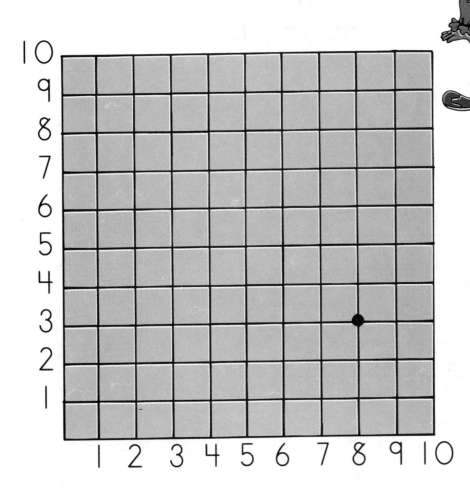

Name: _____

Geometry: Polygons

A polygon is a closed figure with three or more sides.

Directions: Identify the polygons.

Example:

 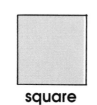 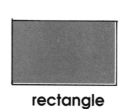   

| **triangle** | **square** | **rectangle** | **pentagon** | **hexagon** | **octagon** |
| 3 sides | 4 equal sides | 4 sides | 5 sides | 6 sides | 8 sides |

_____

_____

_____

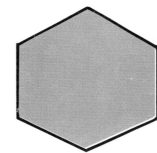

_____

_____

_____

Geometry: Lines, Rays, Segments

A line segment has two end points.

write

A line has no end points and goes on and on in both directions.

write

A ray is part of a line and goes on and on in one direction. It has one end point.

write

Directions: Identify each of the following as a line, line segment, or ray.

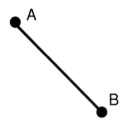

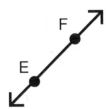

_____   _____   _____

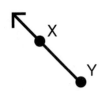

_____   _____

Name: _____

Geometry: Circles

A circle is a round figure. It is named by its center.

A radius is a line segment from the center to any point on the circle.

A diameter is a line segment with both points on the circle. The diameter always passes through the center of the circle.

Directions: Name the radius, diameter, and circle.

Example:

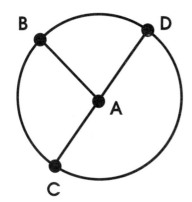

Circle _____A_____

radius _____AB_____

diameter _____DC_____

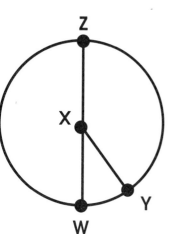

Circle _____

radius _____

diameter _____

Circle _____

radius _____

diameter _____

Name: _____

Review

Directions: Complete the graph using the information in the box.

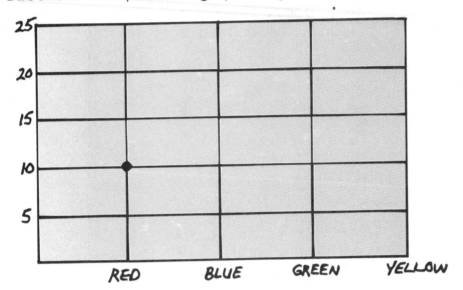

Team	Games Played
Red	10
Blue	20
Green	15
Yellow	25

Directions: Draw a line from the figure to its name.

line

square

segment

radius

octagon

triangle

pentagon

Two's and Three's

Work with a friend.

■ Use 2s and 3s with $+$, $-$, $\times$, or $\div$.

■ Write true number sentences.

Each sentence must have *at least* one 2 and one 3.

1. _____ = 0

2. _____ = 1

3. _____ = 2

4. _____ = 3

5. _____ = 4

6. _____ = 5

7. _____ = 6

8. _____ = 7

9. _____ = 8

10. _____ = 9

$3 - 2 = 1$

$3 \div 3 + 2 - 2 = 1$

$(3 + 2) \div (3 + 2) = 1$

$2 \div 2 \times 3 \div 3 = 1$

Using Mixed Operations with Basic Facts

Digit Derby

Make these number cards.
Find 2 markers.
Ask someone at home to play this game with you.

Mix up the cards and place them face down.

Place the markers in any two squares on the game board.

Take turns.

On each turn:
- Pick a card.
- Move the marker one space horizontally, vertically, or diagonally to a number that has the digit on the card.

0 1 2 3 4 5 6 7 8 9

Game Board

183,426	507,932	391,706
231,849	762,045	918,620
456,195	329,607	584,371
970,584	618,390	842,753

Score:
- 6 points if the digit is in the hundred thousands place.
- 5 points if the digit is in the ten thousands place.
- 4 points if the digit is in the thousands place.
- 3 points if the digit is in the hundreds place.
- 2 points if the digit is in the tens place.
- 1 point if the digit is in the ones place.

After every card has been picked, find the total of the scores.
The winner is the player with the greater total score.

Score Sheet

	Player 1:	Player 2:
Turn 1		
Turn 2		
Turn 3		
Turn 4		
Turn 5		
TOTAL		

Roll and Round

Play this game with a friend.

To Play:

- One player rolls a number cube.

- Both players write the number in one of the boxes on their score sheets.

- After all 16 boxes are filled, players round each number to the nearest thousand.

- Players compare the four rounded numbers, one for one.

To Score:

- Score 1 point for the greater rounded number.

- Score 0 for a tie.

The player with the greater total score is the winner.

Player____				Player____		
Number	Rounded to the nearest thousand	Score		Number	Rounded to the nearest thousand	Score
1.☐☐☐☐				1.☐☐☐☐		
2.☐☐☐☐				2.☐☐☐☐		
3.☐☐☐☐				3.☐☐☐☐		
4.☐☐☐☐				4.☐☐☐☐		
Total				**Total**		

Four In A Line

Here's a game for you and friend.

Rules

- Take turns.
- Pick two numbers from the sign.
- Add the numbers.
- Mark the answer on the game board. Use your **X** or **O**.

The first player with four **X**s or **O**s in a row, column, or diagonal is the winner.

X _____
Player's Name

O _____
Player's Name

47	532
789	111
428	653

GAMEBOARD

836	539	1,217	643
960	FREE	158	1,442
475	900	1,321	1,081
764	700	1,185	579

Adding 2- to 4-Digit Numbers

Difference Delight

Find someone to play this game with you.

Set a time limit: 2 minutes for each rule.

Each player should:

■ Write subtraction examples that fit the rules.

■ Subtract.

■ Check the examples with the other player.

■ Score 1 point for each example that fits the rule.

Player 1	Rule	Player 2
	The difference has 2 digits.	
	The difference is between 500 and 600.	
	The difference has 4 digits.	
	The difference is between 5,000 and 5,050.	
	The difference is 398.	

Total Score_____   Total Score_____

Are You Square?

Some people are **squares**.

Some people are **rectangles**.

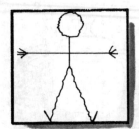
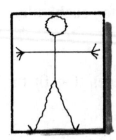

Are you a **square** or a **rectangle**?

Get some string and a pair of scissors.
Find a friend to help.
Cut a piece of string equal to your height.
Cut a piece of string the same length as your outstretched arms.

Compare the pieces of strings.
If they are the same length, you are a **square.**
If not, you are a **rectangle.**

I am a _____.

What about your family?

Use string to find out if the people in your family
are squares or rectangles.

Fill in the table.

Name	Shape

Nonstandard Measureme

Measurement
Estimation

o this activity with a friend.
stimate first.
easure to the nearest inch.
hen ring the closer estimate.

Estimate the length	Your Estimate	Friend's Estimate	Measurement
around your wrist			
of your foot			
from your knee to the floor			
of your thumbnail			
around your ankle			
from your elbow to your shoulder			

Using Customary Units

Tantalizing Toothpicks

Here are some puzzles for you and your family.

- Get some toothpicks.
- Make each diagram.
- Follow the directions.
- Find out how many of these puzzles you can solve in 10 minutes.

You can't leave extra toothpicks.

1. Remove 2 toothpicks.
Leave 3 squares.

2. Remove 4 toothpicks.
Leave 2 squares.

3. Remove 4 toothpicks.
Leave 4 squares.

4. Remove 5 toothpicks.
Leave 4 squares.

5. Remove 8 toothpicks.
Leave 5 squares.

6. Remove 4 toothpicks.
Leave 5 squares.

Score:
5 or 6 puzzles — Superior
3 or 4 puzzles — Very Good
1 or 2 puzzles — Keep Trying

Using Polygo

ANSWER KEY

MASTER MATH
4

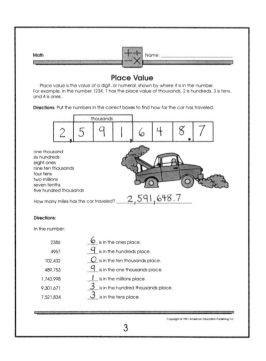

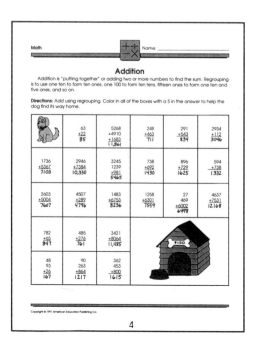

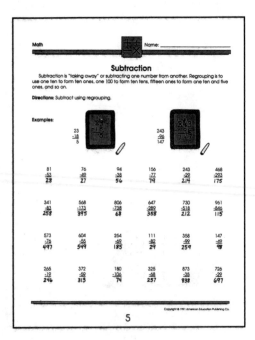

Math Name: _____

Subtraction

Subtraction is "taking away" or subtracting one number from another. Regrouping is to use one ten to form ten ones, one 100 to form ten tens, fifteen ones to form one ten and five ones, and so on.

Directions: Subtract using regrouping.

Examples:

```
  23          243
 -18          -96
   5          147
```

```
 81    76    94   156   243   468
-53   -49   -38   -77   -29  -293
 28    27    56    79   214   175

341   568   806   647   730   961
-83  -173  -738  -289  -518  -846
258   395    68   358   212   115

573   604   254   111   358   147
-76   -55   -69   -82   -99   -49
497   549   185    29   259    98

265   372   180   325   873   726
-19   -59  -106   -68   -35   -29
246   313    74   257   838   697
```

5

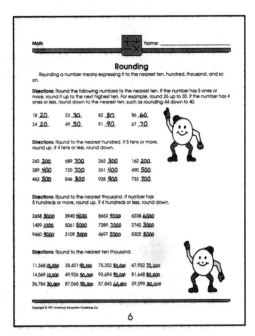

Math Name: _____

Rounding

Rounding a number means expressing it to the nearest ten, hundred, thousand, and so on.

Directions: Round the following numbers to the nearest ten. If the number has 5 ones or more, round it up to the next highest ten. For example, round 26 up to 30. If the number has 4 ones or less, round down to the nearest ten, such as rounding 44 down to 40.

18 _20_   33 _30_   82 _80_   56 _60_
24 _20_   49 _50_   91 _90_   67 _70_

Directions: Round to the nearest hundred. If 5 tens or more, round up. If 4 tens or less, round down.

243 _200_   689 _700_   263 _300_   162 _200_
389 _400_   720 _700_   351 _400_   490 _500_
463 _500_   846 _800_   928 _900_   733 _700_

Directions: Round to the nearest thousand. If number has 5 hundreds or more, round up. If 4 hundreds or less, round down.

2638 _3000_   3940 _4000_   8653 _9000_   6238 _6000_
1429 _1000_   5061 _5000_   7289 _7000_   2742 _3000_
9460 _9000_   3109 _3000_   4697 _5000_   8302 _8000_

Directions: Round to the nearest ten thousand.

11,368 _10,000_   38,421 _40,000_   75,302 _80,000_   67,932 _70,000_
14,569 _10,000_   49,926 _50,000_   93,694 _90,000_   81,648 _80,000_
26,784 _30,000_   87,065 _90,000_   57,843 _60,000_   29,399 _30,000_

6

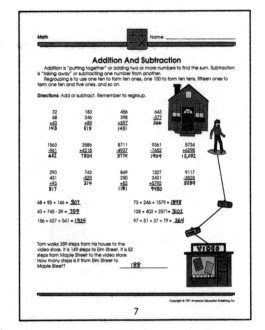

Math Name: _____

Addition And Subtraction

Addition is "putting together" or adding two or more numbers to find the sum. Subtraction is "taking away" or subtracting one number from another.

Regrouping is to use one ten to form ten ones, one 100 to form ten tens, fifteen ones to form one ten and five ones, and so on.

Directions: Add or subtract. Remember to regroup.

```
 32    183   456   643
 68    246   398  -377
+43   +89   +597   266
143   519   1451
```

```
1563   3586   8711   9361   5734
-941  +4218  -4937  -7452  +6298
 622   7804   3774   1909  12,032
```

```
293   743   849   1227   9117
431  -529   260   2431  -3828
+93   214   +82  +5792   5289
817         1181   9450
```

68 + 93 + 146 = _307_
43 + 745 − 29 = _759_
156 + 627 + 541 = _1324_

73 + 246 + 1579 = _1898_
128 + 403 + 2571 = _3102_
97 + 51 + 37 + 79 = _264_

Tom walks 389 steps from his house to the video store. It is 149 steps to Elm Street. It is 52 steps from Maple Street to the video store. How many steps is it from Elm Street to Maple Street? _188_

7

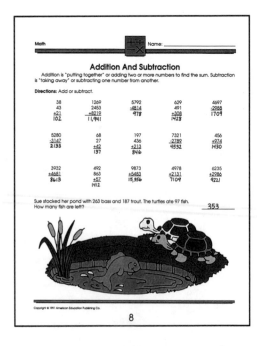

Math Name: _____

Addition And Subtraction

Addition is "putting together" or adding two or more numbers to find the sum. Subtraction is "taking away" or subtracting one number from another.

Directions: Add or subtract.

```
  38   1269   5792    629   4697
  43   2453  -4814    491  -2988
 +21  +8219    978   +308   1709
 102  11,941         1428
```

```
5280     68    197   7321    456
-3147     27    436  -2789   +974
2133    +42   +213   4532   1430
        137    846
```

```
3932    492   9873   4978   6235
+4681   863  +5483  +2131  +2986
8613   +57   15,356  7109   9221
       1412
```

Sue stocked her pond with 263 bass and 187 trout. The turtles ate 97 fish. How many fish are left? _353_

8

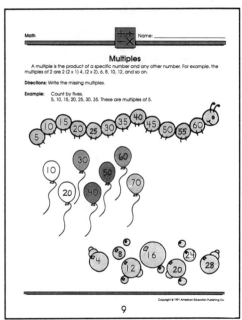

Math Name: _____

Multiples

A multiple is the product of a specific number and any other number. For example, the multiples of 2 are 2 (2 x 1) 4, (2 x 2), 6, 8, 10, 12, and so on.

Directions: Write the missing multiples.

Example: Count by fives.
5, 10, 15, 20, 25, 30, 35. These are multiples of 5.

5 10 15 20 25 30 35 40 45 50 55 60

10 20 30 40 50 60 70

4 8 12 16 20 24 28

9

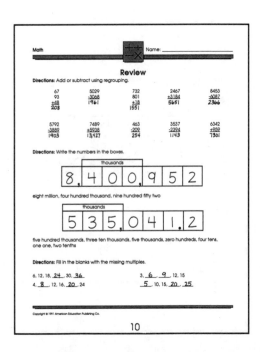

Math Name: _____

Review

Directions: Add or subtract using regrouping.

```
 67   5029   732   2467   8453
 93  -3068   801  +3184  -6087
+48   1961   +18   5651   2366
208          1551
```

```
5792   7489   463   3537   6342
-3889  +5938  -209  -2394   +959
1903  13,427  254   1143   7301
```

Directions: Write the numbers in the boxes.

		thousands					
8,	4	0	0,	9	5	2	

eight million, four hundred thousand, nine hundred fifty two

		thousands					
5	3	5,	0	4	1 .	2	

five hundred thousands, three ten thousands, five thousands, zero hundreds, four tens, one one, two tenths

Directions: Fill in the blanks with the missing multiples.

6, 12, 18, _24_, 30, _36_
4, _8_, 12, 16, _20_, 24

3, _6_, _9_, 12, 15
_5_, 10, 15, _20_, _25_

10

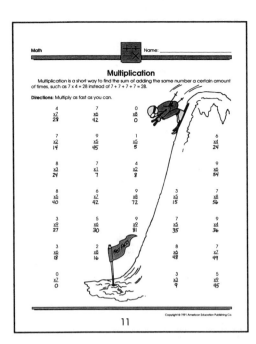

Multiplication

Multiplication is a short way to find the sum of adding the same number a certain amount of times, such as 7 x 4 = 28 instead of 7 + 7 + 7 + 7 = 28.

Directions: Multiply as fast as you can.

```
  4        7        0
 x7       x6       x8
 28       42        0

  7        9        1                6
 x2       x5       x5               x4
 14       45        5               24

  8        7        4                9
 x3       x1       x2               x6
 24        7        8               54

  8        6        9        3       7
 x5       x7       x8       x5      x8
 40       42       72       15      56

  3        5        9        7       9
 x9       x6       x9       x5      x4
 27       30       81       35      36

  3        2        8                7
 x6       x8       x6               x7
 18       16       48               49

  0                                  3       5
 x7                                 x3      x9
  0                                  9      45
```

11

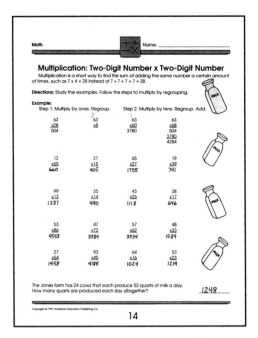

Multiplication: Two-Digit Number x Two-Digit Number

Multiplication is a short way to find the sum of adding the same number a certain amount of times, such as 7 x 4 = 28 instead of 7 + 7 + 7 + 7 = 28.

Directions: Study the examples. Follow the steps to multiply by regrouping.

Example:

Step 1. Multiply by ones. Regroup.　　Step 2. Multiply by tens. Regroup. Add.

```
              2
  63         63         63          63
 x28        x8         x60         x08
 504                   3780        504
                                  3780
                                  4284
```

```
  12        27        65        19
 x55       x15       x27       x39
 660       405      1755       741

  99        35        43        38
 x13       x14       x26       x17
1287       490      1118       646

  53        47        57        48
 x86       x72       x62       x33
4558      3384      3534      1584

  27        93        64        53
 x54       x45       x16       x23
1458      4185      1024      1219
```

The Jones farm has 24 cows that each produce 52 quarts of milk a day. How many quarts are produced each day altogether?　　1248

14

Multiplication: Tens, Hundreds, And Thousands

Multiplication is a short way to find the sum of adding the same number a certain amount of times, such as 7 x 4 = 28 instead of 7 + 7 + 7 + 7 = 28.

Directions: Study the examples.

Examples:

When multiplying a number by 10, the answer is the number with a zero. It is like counting by 10s.

```
 10     10     10     10     10     10
 x1     x2     x3     x4     x5     x6
 10     20     30     40     50     60
```

When multiplying a number by 100, the answer is the number with two zeroes. When multiplying a number by 1000, the answer is the number with three zeroes.

```
100    100    100   1000   1000   1000
 x1     x2     x3     x1     x2     x3
100    200    300   1000   2000   3000
```

Such basic facts help us multiply.

```
  4    400       8    800      7    700
 x2     x2      x3     x3     x5     x5
  8    800      24   2400     35   3,500
```

Directions: Multiply.

```
 10     60     400    700     50
 x3     x5      x5     x8     x7
 30    300    2000   5600    350

 80   4000    6000    300    700
 x9     x2      x4     x9     x6
720   9000  24,000   2700   4200
```

3 x 800 = 2400　　　9 x 2000 = 18,000　　　7 x 90 = 630

12

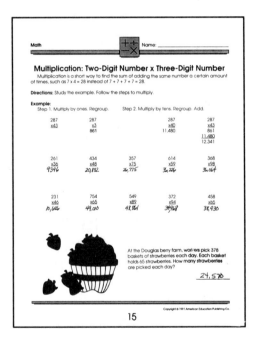

Multiplication: Two-Digit Number x Three-Digit Number

Multiplication is a short way to find the sum of adding the same number a certain amount of times, such as 7 x 4 = 28 instead of 7 + 7 + 7 + 7 = 28.

Directions: Study the example. Follow the steps to multiply.

Example:

Step 1. Multiply by ones. Regroup.　　Step 2. Multiply by tens. Regroup. Add.

```
 287        287         287
 x43        x3          x43
            861         861
                     11,480
                     11,480
                     12,341
```

```
 261       434       357       614       368
 x36       x48       x75       x59       x98
9396    29,832    26,775    36,226    36,064

 231       754       549       372       458
 x46       x65       x89       x94       x85
10,626   49,010    48,861    34,968    38,930
```

At the Douglas berry farm, workers pick 378 baskets of strawberries each day. Each basket holds 65 strawberries. How many strawberries are picked each day?　　24,570

15

Multiplication: One-Digit Number x Two-Digit Number

Multiplication is a short way to find the sum of adding the same number a certain amount of times, such as 7 x 4 = 28 instead of 7 + 7 + 7 + 7 = 28.

Directions: Study the example. Follow the steps to multiplying by regrouping tens.

Example:

Step 1. Multiply ones. Regroup.　　Step 2. Multiply Tens. Add 2 tens.

```
   2            2
  54           54
  x7           x7
   8          378
```

```
 27     63     52     91     45
 x3     x4     x5     x9     x7
 81    252    260    819    315

 75     64     76     93     87
 x2     x5     x3     x6     x4
150    320    228    558    348

 66     38     47     64     51
 x7     x2     x8     x9     x8
462     76    376    576    408

 99     13     32     25     15
 x3     x7     x4     x8     x7
297     91    128    200    105
```

The chickens on the Smith farm produce 48 dozen eggs each day. How many dozen eggs do they produce in 7 days?　　336

13

75

Multiplication: Three-Digit Number x Three-Digit Number

Multiplication is a short way to find the sum of adding the same number a certain amount of times, such as 7 x 4 = 28 instead of 7 + 7 + 7 + 7 = 28.

Directions: Multiply. Regroup when needed.

Example:

```
   563
  x248
  4504
  2252
 1126
139,624
```

Hint: When multiplying by the tens, start writing the number in the tens place. When multiplying by the hundreds, start in the hundreds place.

```
 842       932       759       531
x167      x272      x468      x556
140,614  253,504   355,212   295,236

 383       523       229       738
x476      x349      x189      x513
182,308  182,527    43,281   378,594

 483       946       365
x148      x367      x622
71,484   347,182   227,030
```

James grows pumpkins on his farm. He has 362 rows of pumpkins. There are 593 pumpkins in each row. How many pumpkins does James grow?　　214,666

16

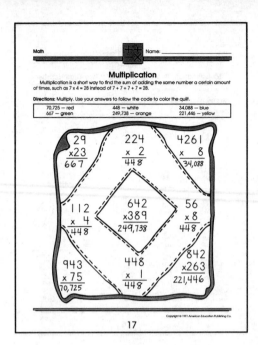

Multiplication

Multiplication is a short way to find the sum of adding the same number a certain amount of times, such as 7 x 4 = 28 instead of 7 + 7 + 7 + 7 = 28.

Directions: Multiply. Use your answers to follow the code to color the quilt.

| 70,725 — red | 448 — white | 34,088 — blue |
| 667 — green | 249,738 — orange | 221,446 — yellow |

$$29 \times 23 = 667$$
$$224 \times 2 = 448$$
$$4261 \times 8 = 34,088$$
$$112 \times 4 = 448$$
$$642 \times 389 = 249,738$$
$$56 \times 8 = 448$$
$$943 \times 75 = 70,725$$
$$448 \times 1 = 448$$
$$842 \times 263 = 221,446$$

Copyright © 1991 American Education Publishing Co.

17

Review

Directions: Multiply. Work the problem in the box. Color the ribbons blue if the answer is correct.

$$5683 \times 9 = 51,147$$
$$256 \times 38 = 9728$$
$$489 \times 56 = 27,384$$
$$356 \times 427 = 152,012$$
$$800 \times 7 = 5600$$
$$60 \times 5 = 300$$

Copyright © 1991 American Education Publishing Co.

18

Division

Division is a way to find out how many times one number is contained in another number. For example, 28 ÷ 7 = 4 means that there are four groups of seven in 28.

Directions: Study the example. Then divide to solve the problems. Remember that the remainder must be smaller than the divisor.

Example:

$$7)\overline{860} = 122\,r6 \qquad 6)\overline{611} = 101\,r5 \qquad 8)\overline{279} = 34\,r7 \qquad 4)\overline{338} = 84\,r2 \qquad 6)\overline{979} = 163\,r1$$

$$3)\overline{792} = 264 \qquad 5)\overline{463} = 92\,r3 \qquad 6)\overline{940} = 156\,r4 \qquad 4)\overline{647} = 161\,r3 \qquad 3)\overline{814} = 271\,r1$$

$$7)\overline{758} = 108\,r2 \qquad 5)\overline{356} = 71\,r1 \qquad 4)\overline{276} = 69 \qquad 8)\overline{328} = 41 \qquad 9)\overline{306} = 34$$

The record store has 491 records. The store sells 8 records a day. How many days will it take to sell all of the records?   61 r 3

Copyright © 1991 American Education Publishing Co.

19

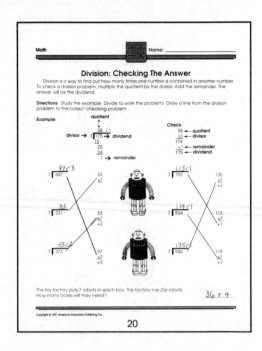

Division: Checking The Answer

Division is a way to find out how many times one number is contained in another number. To check a division problem, multiply the quotient by the divisor. Add the remainder. The answer will be the dividend.

Directions: Study the example. Divide to work the problems. Draw a line from the division problem to the correct checking problem.

The toy factory puts 7 robots in each box. The factory has 256 robots. How many boxes will they need?   36 r 4

Copyright © 1991 American Education Publishing Co.

20

Division: 1-Digit Divisor

Division is a way to find out how many times one number is contained in another number.

Directions: Work the problems on another sheet of paper. Use the code to color the picture.

Color these answers:

5)895 (A=179)	6)493 (A=82 r1)	6)940 (A=156 r4)	4)647 (A=161 r3)	orange
4)672 (A=168)	6)696 (A=116)	5)749 (A=149 r4)	6)628 (A=78 r4)	blue
3)814 (A=271 r1)	7)490 (A=70)	5)398 (A=79 r3)	2)571 (A=285 r1)	black

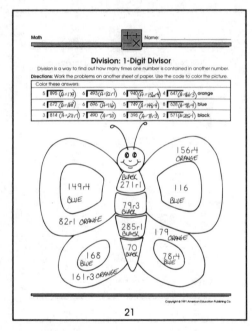

Copyright © 1991 American Education Publishing Co.

21

Division: 2-Digit Divisor

Division is a way to find out how many times one number is contained in another number.

Directions: Study the example. Divide. Remember to check your answer by multiplying it by the divisor and adding the remainder.

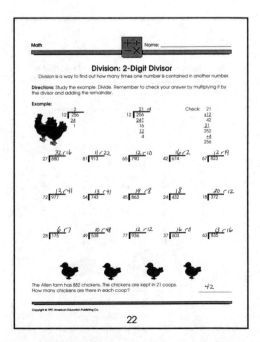

Example:

$$27)\overline{880} = 32\,r16 \qquad 81)\overline{913} = 11\,r22 \qquad 65)\overline{790} = 12\,r10 \qquad 42)\overline{674} = 16\,r2 \qquad 67)\overline{823} = 12\,r19$$

$$72)\overline{977} = 13\,r41 \qquad 54)\overline{743} = 13\,r41 \qquad 45)\overline{863} = 19\,r8 \qquad 24)\overline{432} = 18 \qquad 18)\overline{372} = 20\,r12$$

$$28)\overline{175} = 6\,r7 \qquad 49)\overline{538} = 10\,r48 \qquad 77)\overline{936} = 12\,r12 \qquad 37)\overline{603} = 16\,r11 \qquad 63)\overline{835} = 13\,r16$$

The Allen farm has 882 chickens. The chickens are kept in 21 coops. How many chickens are there in each coop?   42

Copyright © 1991 American Education Publishing Co.

22

Page 23

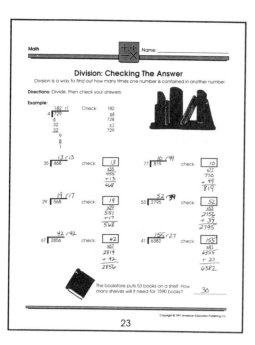

Math Name: _____

Division: Checking The Answer

Division is a way to find out how many times one number is contained in another number.

Directions: Divide, then check your answers.

Example:

$$4\overline{)729} = 182\ r1$$

Check:
182
×4
728
+1
729

$$35\overline{)468} = 13\ r13$$ check: 13 ×35 455 +13 468

$$77\overline{)819} = 10\ r49$$ check: 10 ×77 770 +49 819

$$29\overline{)568} = 19\ r17$$ check: 19 ×29 551 +17 568

$$53\overline{)2795} = 52\ r39$$ check: 52 ×53 2756 +39 2795

$$67\overline{)2856} = 42\ r42$$ check: 42 ×67 2814 +42 2856

$$41\overline{)6382} = 155\ r27$$ check: 155 ×41 6355 +27 6382

The bookstore puts 53 books on a shelf. How many shelves will it need for 1590 books? __30__

Copyright © 1991 American Education Publishing Co.

23

Page 24

Math Name: _____

Averaging

An average is found by adding two or more quantities and then dividing by the number of quantities.

Directions: Study the example. Find the sum and divide by the number of quantities. Draw a line from each problem to the correct average.

Example:
24+36+30=90÷3
90 ÷ 3=30 Average

$$3\overline{)90} = 30\ \text{Average}$$

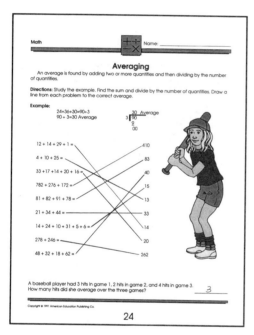

12 + 14 + 29 + 1 =   410
4 + 10 + 25 =   83
33 +17 +14 + 20 + 16 =   40
782 + 276 + 172 =   15
81 + 82 + 91 + 78 =   13
21 + 34 + 44 =   33
14 + 24 + 10 + 31 + 5 + 6 = 14
278 + 246 =   20
48 + 32 + 18 + 62 =   262

A baseball player had 3 hits in game 1, 2 hits in game 2, and 4 hits in game 3. How many hits did she average over the three games? __3__

Copyright © 1991 American Education Publishing Co.

24

Page 25

Math Name: _____

Averaging

An average is found by adding two or more quantities and then dividing by the number of quantities.

Directions: Find the averages.

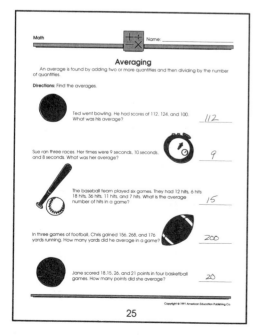

Ted went bowling. He had scores of 112, 124, and 100. What was his average? __112__

Sue ran three races. Her times were 9 seconds, 10 seconds, and 8 seconds. What was her average? __9__

The baseball team played six games. They had 12 hits, 6 hits, 18 hits, 36 hits, 11 hits, and 7 hits. What is the average number of hits in a game? __15__

In three games of football, Chris gained 156, 268, and 176 yards running. How many yards did he average in a game? __200__

Jane scored 18, 15, 26, and 21 points in four basketball games. How many points did she average? __20__

Copyright © 1991 American Education Publishing Co.

25

Page 26

Math Name: _____

Review

Directions: Divide.

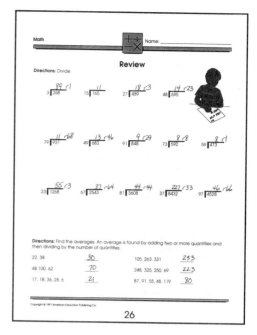

$$3\overline{)268} = 89\ r1$$
$$15\overline{)165} = 11$$
$$27\overline{)489} = 18\ r3$$
$$48\overline{)695} = 14\ r23$$

$$79\overline{)937} = 11\ r68$$
$$49\overline{)683} = 13\ r46$$
$$91\overline{)848} = 9\ r29$$
$$73\overline{)592} = 8\ r8$$
$$59\overline{)473} = 8\ r1$$

$$23\overline{)1268} = 55\ r3$$
$$67\overline{)2543} = 37\ r64$$
$$81\overline{)3608} = 44\ r44$$
$$37\overline{)8432} = 227\ r33$$
$$97\overline{)4528} = 46\ r46$$

Directions: Find the averages. An average is found by adding two or more quantities and then dividing by the number of quantities.

22, 38   __30__   105, 263, 331   __233__
48, 100, 62   __70__   248, 325, 250, 69 __223__
17, 18, 36, 28, 6 __21__   87, 91, 55, 48, 119 __80__

Copyright © 1991 American Education Publishing Co.

26

Page 27

Math Name: _____

Fraction: Addition

A fraction is a number that names part of a whole, such as 1/2 or 1/3. The denominator is the bottom number in a fraction; the numerator is the top number.
When adding fractions with the same denominator, the denominator stays the same. Add only the numerators.

Example:
numerator → 1 + 2 = 3
denominator → 8   8   8

Directions: Study the example. Add the fractions. The first one is done for you.

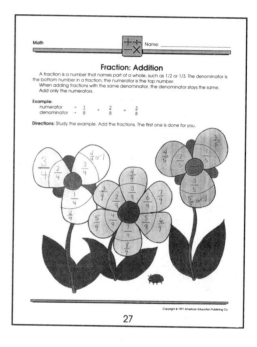

Copyright © 1991 American Education Publishing Co.

27

Page 28

Math Name: _____

Fractions: Subtraction

A fraction is a number that names part of a whole, such as 1/2 or 1/3. The denominator is the bottom number in a fraction; the numerator is the top number.
When subtracting fractions with the same denominator, the denominator stays the same. Subtract only the numerators.

Directions: Solve the problems below, working from left to right across each row. As you find each answer, copy the letter from the code box into the numbered blanks. The first one is done for you. The answer will tell the name of a famous American.

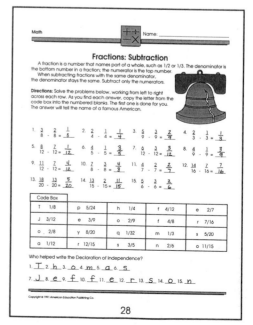

1. $\frac{3}{8} - \frac{2}{8} = \frac{1}{8}$ 2. $\frac{5}{4} - \frac{4}{4} = \frac{1}{4}$ 3. $\frac{5}{9} - \frac{2}{9} = \frac{3}{9}$ 4. $\frac{2}{3} - \frac{1}{3} = \frac{1}{3}$

5. $\frac{8}{12} - \frac{7}{12} = \frac{1}{12}$ 6. $\frac{4}{5} - \frac{1}{5} = \frac{3}{5}$ 7. $\frac{6}{9} - \frac{3}{9} = \frac{3}{9}$ 8. $\frac{4}{9} - \frac{1}{9} = \frac{3}{9}$

9. $\frac{11}{12} - \frac{7}{12} = \frac{4}{12}$ 10. $\frac{7}{8} - \frac{3}{8} = \frac{4}{8}$ 11. $\frac{4}{7} - \frac{2}{7} = \frac{2}{7}$ 12. $\frac{14}{16} - \frac{7}{16} = \frac{7}{16}$

13. $\frac{18}{20} - \frac{13}{20} = \frac{5}{20}$ 14. $\frac{13}{15} - \frac{2}{15} = \frac{11}{15}$ 15. $\frac{5}{6} - \frac{3}{6} = \frac{2}{6}$

Code Box			
T 1/8	p 5/24	h 1/4	f 4/12	e 2/7
J 3/12	e 3/9	o 2/9	f 4/8	r 7/16
o 2/8	y 8/20	q 1/32	m 1/3	s 5/20
a 1/12	r 12/15	s 3/5	n 2/6	o 11/15

Who helped write the Declaration of Independence?

1. __T__ __h__ __o__ __m__ __a__ __s__

7. __J__ __e__ __f__ 10. __f__ __e__ __r__ __s__ 14. __o__ __n__

Copyright © 1991 American Education Publishing Co.

28

77

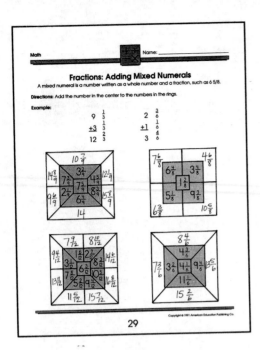

Fractions: Adding Mixed Numerals

A mixed numeral is a number written as a whole number and a fraction, such as 6 5/8.

Directions: Add the number in the center to the numbers in the rings.

Example:

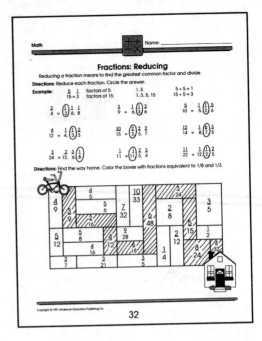

Fractions: Reducing

Reducing a fraction means to find the greatest common factor and divide.

Directions: Reduce each fraction. Circle the answer.

Example:

Directions: Find the way home. Color the boxes with fractions equivalent to 1/8 and 1/3.

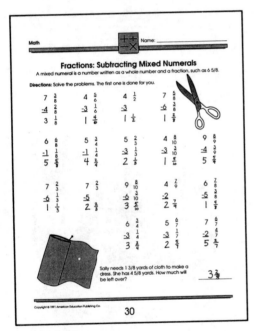

Fractions: Subtracting Mixed Numerals

A mixed numeral is a number written as a whole number and a fraction, such as 6 5/8.

Directions: Solve the problems. The first one is done for you.

Sally needs 1 3/8 yards of cloth to make a dress. She has 4 5/8 yards. How much will be left over?   3 2/8

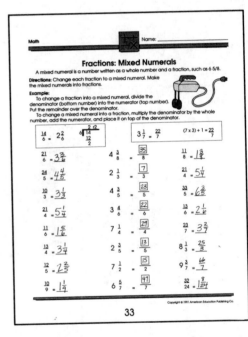

Fractions: Mixed Numerals

A mixed numeral is a number written as a whole number and a fraction, such as 6 5/8.

Directions: Change each fraction to a mixed numeral. Make the mixed numerals into fractions.

Example:
To change a fraction into a mixed numeral, divide the denominator (bottom number) into the numerator (top number). Put the remainder over the denominator.
To change a mixed numeral into a fraction, multiply the denominator by the whole number, add the numerator, and place it on top of the denominator.

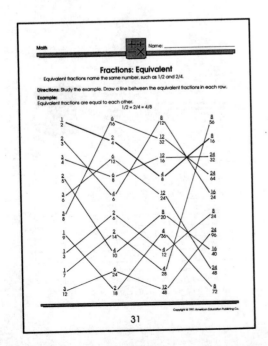

Fractions: Equivalent

Equivalent fractions name the same number, such as 1/2 and 2/4.

Directions: Study the example. Draw a line between the equivalent fractions in each row.

Example:
Equivalent fractions are equal to each other.
1/2 = 2/4 = 4/8

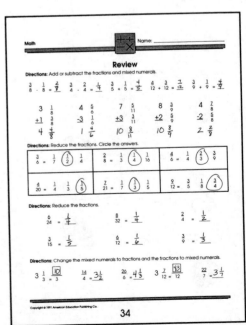

Review

Directions: Add or subtract the fractions and mixed numerals.

Directions: Reduce the fractions. Circle the answers.

Directions: Reduce the fractions.

Directions: Change the mixed numerals to fractions and the fractions to mixed numerals.

Decimals

A decimal is a number with one or more places to the right of a decimal point, such as 6.5 or 2.25. A decimal point is the dot between the ones place and the tenths place.

Directions: Add or subtract. Remember to include the decimal point in your answer.

Example:
13/10 = 1.3   16/10 = 1.6
1.3 +1.6 = 2.9

8.1 +1.7 = 9.8	4.1 +6.2 = 10.3	0.5 +1.6 = 2.1	7.6 -6.5 = 1.1	7.2 -2.6 = 4.6	1.2 +5.0 = 6.2
8.7 -3.9 = 4.8	6.8 -3.7 = 3.1	7.8 -6.8 = 1.0	16.5 -7.3 = 9.2	6.4 +5.3 = 11.7	10.0 +3.5 = 13.5
.42 +.35 = .77	.98 -.87 = .11	.78 -.13 = .65	.83 +.12 = .95	.95 -.14 = .81	3.23 +2.48 = 5.71
4.68 -2.65 = 2.03	5.86 -2.73 = 3.13	6.98 +1.40 = 8.38	3.27 +1.82 = 5.09	4.65 -1.32 = 3.33	5.97 +2.77 = 8.74

Mr. Martin went on a car trip with his family. Mr. Martin purchased gas three times. He bought 6.7 gallons, 7.3 gallons, then 5.8 gallons of gas. How much gas did he purchase in all? 19.8 gallons

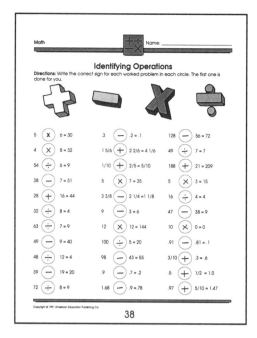

Identifying Operations

Directions: Write the correct sign for each worked problem in each circle. The first one is done for you.

5 (×) 6 = 30	.3 (−) .2 = .1	128 (−) 56 = 72
4 (×) 8 = 32	1 5/6 (+) 2 2/6 = 4 1/6	49 (÷) 7 = 7
54 (÷) 6 = 9	1/10 (+) 2/5 = 5/10	188 (+) 21 = 209
38 (−) 7 = 31	5 (×) 7 = 35	5 (×) 3 = 15
28 (+) 16 = 44	3 3/8 (−) 2 1/4 = 1 1/8	16 (÷) 4 = 4
32 (÷) 8 = 4	9 (−) 3 = 6	47 (−) 38 = 9
63 (÷) 7 = 9	12 (×) 12 = 144	10 (×) 0 = 0
49 (−) 9 = 40	100 (÷) 5 = 20	.91 (−) .81 = .1
48 (÷) 12 = 4	98 (−) 43 = 55	3/10 (+) .3 = .6
39 (−) 19 = 20	.9 (−) .7 = .2	.5 (÷) 1/2 = 1.0
72 (÷) 8 = 9	1.68 (−) .9 = .78	.97 (+) 5/10 = 1.47

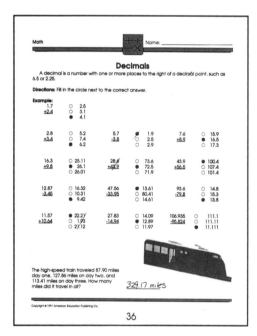

Decimals

A decimal is a number with one or more places to the right of a decimal point, such as 6.5 or 2.25.

Directions: Fill in the circle next to the correct answer.

Example:
1.7 +2.4 → ○ 2.5 ○ 3.1 ● 4.1

2.8 +3.4 → ○ 5.2 ○ 7.4 ● 6.2
5.7 -3.8 → ● 1.9 ○ 2.5 ○ 2.9
7.6 +8.9 → ○ 15.9 ● 16.5 ○ 17.3

16.3 +9.8 → ○ 25.11 ● 26.1 ○ 26.01
28.6 +43.9 → ○ 73.6 ● 72.5 ○ 71.9
43.9 +56.5 → ● 100.4 ○ 107.4 ○ 101.4

12.87 -3.45 → ○ 16.32 ○ 10.31 ● 9.42
47.56 -33.95 → ● 13.61 ○ 80.41 ○ 14.61
93.6 -79.8 → ○ 14.8 ○ 15.3 ● 13.8

11.57 +10.64 → ● 22.21 ○ 1.98 ○ 21.12
27.83 -14.94 → ○ 14.09 ● 12.89 ○ 11.97
106.935 -95.824 → ○ 111.1 ● 111.11 ○ 111.111

The high-speed train traveled 87.90 miles day one, 127.86 miles on day two, and 113.41 miles on day three. How many miles did it travel in all? 329.17 miles

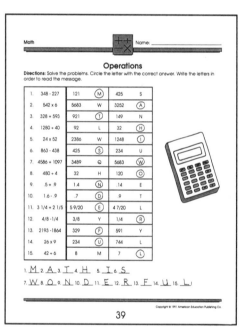

Operations

Directions: Solve the problems. Circle the letter with the correct answer. Write the letters in order to read the message.

1.	348 - 227	121 (M)	425	S
2.	542 × 6	5683	W	3252 (A)
3.	328 + 593	921 (T)	149	N
4.	1280 ÷ 40	92	L	32 (H)
5.	24 × 52	2386	W	1248 (I)
6.	863 - 438	425 (S)	234	U
7.	4586 + 1097	3489	Q	5683 (W)
8.	480 ÷ 4	32	H	120 (O)
9.	.5 + .9	1.4 (N)	.14	E
10.	1.6 - .9	.7 (D)	.9	T
11.	3 1/4 + 2 1/5	5 9/20		4 7/20 (E)
12.	4/8 - 1/4	3/8	Y	1/4 (R)
13.	2193 - 1864	329 (F)	591	Y
14.	26 × 9	234 (U)	744	L
15.	42 ÷ 6	8	M	7 (L)

1. M 2. A 3. T 4. H 5. I 6. S
7. W 8. O 9. N 10. D 11. E 12. R 13. F 14. U 15. L

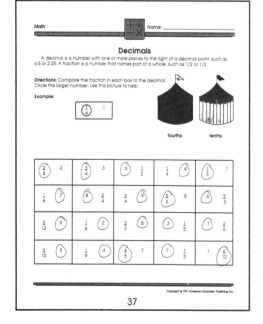

Decimals

A decimal is a number with one or more places to the right of a decimal point, such as 6.5 or 2.25. A fraction is a number that names part of a whole, such as 1/2 or 1/3.

Directions: Compare the fraction in each box to the decimal. Circle the larger number. Use this picture to help.

Example: (1/4) .1

fourths   tenths

(2/4) .2	(3/4) .3	.6 (1/2)	1/4 (.4)	(1/3) .3
1/4 (.7)	(8/...) .5	3/4 (.4)	(9/...) .5	2/5 (.6)
3/12 (.9)	1/6 (.6)	(3/4) .3	(7/...) .5	2/5 (.6)
3/10 (.5)	1/9 (.9)	4/5 (.6)	(1/3) .1	.7 (6/12)

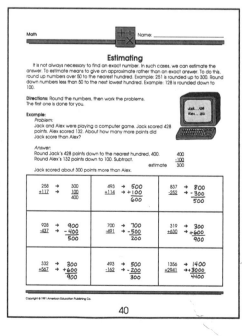

Estimating

It is not always necessary to find an exact number. In such cases, we can estimate the answer. To estimate means to give an approximate rather than an exact answer. To do this, round up numbers over 50 to the nearest hundred. Example: 251 is rounded up to 300. Round down numbers less than 50 to the next lowest hundred. Example: 128 is rounded down to 100.

Directions: Round the numbers, then work the problems. The first one is done for you.

Example:
Problem:
Jack and Alex were playing a computer game. Jack scored 428 points. Alex scored 132. About how many more points did Jack score than Alex?

Answer:
Round Jack's 428 points down to the nearest hundred, 400. Round Alex's 132 points down to 100. Subtract.

400 -100 = 300 estimate

Jack scored about 300 points more than Alex.

258 +117 → 300 +100 = 400	493 +114 → 500 +100 = 600	837 -252 → 800 -300 = 500
928 -437 → 900 -400 = 500	700 -491 → 700 -500 = 200	319 +630 → 300 +600 = 900
332 +567 → 300 +600 = 900	493 -162 → 500 -200 = 300	1356 +2941 → 1400 +3000 = 4400

Estimating

To estimate means to give an approximate rather than an exact answer. Estimating can help us in many ways. One way is planning time.

Directions: Follow the steps to estimate the time it will take to read a book.

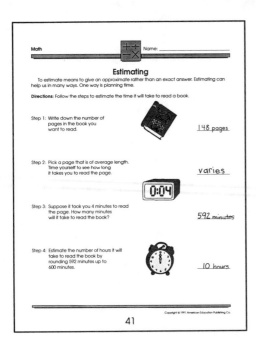

Step 1: Write down the number of pages in the book you want to read.

148 pages

Step 2: Pick a page that is of average length. Time yourself to see how long it takes you to read the page.

varies

Step 3: Suppose it took you 4 minutes to read the page. How many minutes will it take to read the book?

592 minutes

Step 4: Estimate the number of hours it will take to read the book by rounding 592 minutes up to 600 minutes.

10 hours

41

Measurement: Fractions Of An Inch

An inch is a measurement of length in the customary system. It is this long:
Directions: Use a ruler to measure to the nearest quarter of an inch.

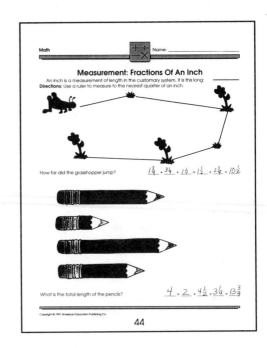

How far did the grasshopper jump? $1\frac{3}{4} + 3\frac{1}{4} + 1\frac{1}{4} + 1\frac{1}{2} + 2\frac{3}{4} = 10\frac{1}{2}$

What is the total length of the pencils? $4 + 2 + 4\frac{1}{2} + 3\frac{1}{4} = 13\frac{3}{4}$

44

Review

Directions: Add or subtract to find the answer.

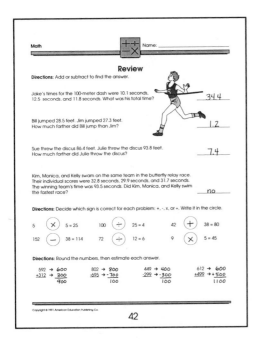

Jake's times for the 100-meter dash were 10.1 seconds, 12.5 seconds, and 11.8 seconds. What was his total time? _34.4_

Bill jumped 28.5 feet. Jim jumped 27.3 feet. How much farther did Bill jump than Jim? _1.2_

Sue threw the discus 86.4 feet. Julie threw the discus 93.8 feet. How much farther did Julie throw the discus? _7.4_

Kim, Monica, and Kelly swam on the same team in the butterfly relay race. Their individual scores were 32.8 seconds, 29.9 seconds, and 31.7 seconds. The winning team's time was 93.5 seconds. Did Kim, Monica, and Kelly swim the fastest race? _no_

Directions: Decide which sign is correct for each problem: +, -, x, or ÷. Write it in the circle.

5 $\times$ 5 = 25   100 $\div$ 25 = 4   42 $+$ 38 = 80

152 $-$ 38 = 114   72 $\div$ 12 = 6   9 $\times$ 5 = 45

Directions: Round the numbers, then estimate each answer.

592 → 600	802 → 800	449 → 400	612 → 600
+312 → +300	-695 → -700	-299 → -300	+499 → +500
900	100	100	1100

42

Measurement: Foot, Yard, Mile

Directions: Choose the measure of distance you would use for each object.

1 foot = 12 inches
1 yard = 3 feet
1 mile = 1760 yards

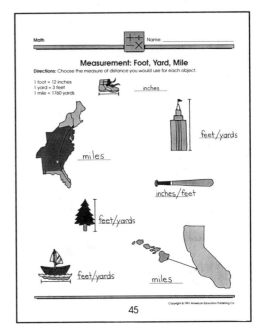

inches

feet/yards

miles

inches/feet

feet/yards

feet/yards

miles

45

Measurement: Inches

An inch is a measurement of length in the customary system. It is this long: _____ .

Directions: Use a ruler to measure each foot to the nearest inch.

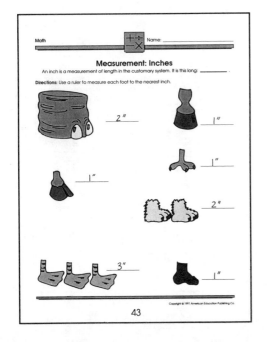

_2"_

_1"_

_1"_

_1"_

_2"_

_3"_

_1"_

43

Measurement: Perimeter And Area

The perimeter is the distance around a figure. The perimeter is found by adding the lengths of the sides.
The area is the number of square units needed to cover a region. The area is found by adding the number of square units. A unit can be any unit of measure. Most often inches, feet, or yards are used.

Directions: Find the perimeter and area for each figure. The first one is done for you.

☐ = 1 square unit

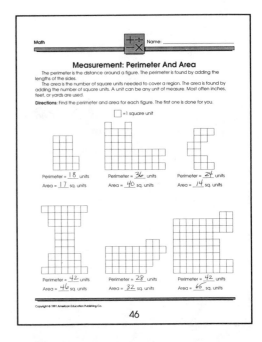

Perimeter = _18_ units
Area = _17_ sq. units

Perimeter = _36_ units
Area = _40_ sq. units

Perimeter = _24_ units
Area = _14_ sq. units

Perimeter = _42_ units
Area = _46_ sq. units

Perimeter = _28_ units
Area = _32_ sq. units

Perimeter = _42_ units
Area = _65_ sq. units

46

Volume

Volume is the number of cubic units that fit inside a figure.

Directions: Find the volume of each figure. The first one is done for you.

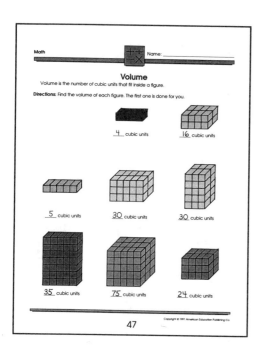

4 cubic units   16 cubic units

5 cubic units   30 cubic units   30 cubic units

35 cubic units   75 cubic units   24 cubic units

47

Review

Directions: Find the perimeter and area. The perimeter is found by adding the lengths of the sides. The area is found by adding the number of square units.

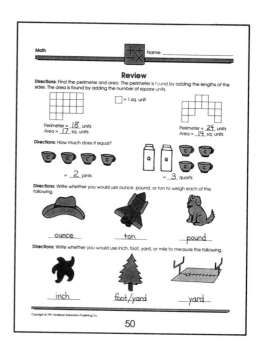

☐ = 1 sq. unit

Perimeter = 18 units
Area = 17 sq. units

Perimeter = 24 units
Area = 14 sq. units

Directions: How much does it equal?

= 2 pints

= 3 quarts

Directions: Write whether you would use ounce, pound, or ton to weigh each of the following.

ounce   ton   pound

Directions: Write whether you would use inch, foot, yard, or mile to measure the following.

inch   foot/yard   yard

50

Measurement: Ounce, Pound, Ton

Directions: Decide whether to use ounces, pounds, or tons to weigh each of the following.

ounce   pound   ton

16 ounces = 1 pound
2000 pounds = 1 ton

ounces   pounds

pounds   ounces

ounces   pounds

tons   tons/pounds

48

Measurement: Centimeters

A centimeter is a measurement of length in the metric system. You can write **cm.** for centimeter.

Directions: Use a centimeter ruler to measure the foot of each animal to the nearest centimeter.

5cm   2cm

2cm   2½ cm each

2½ cm each   2 cm

51

Measurement: Cup, Pint, Quart, Gallon

The cup, pint, quart, and gallon are units in the customary system for measuring liquids.

Directions: Circle the number of objects on the right side of the problem that equal the same amount as the objects on the left. The first one is done for you.

2 cups = 1 pint
2 pints = 1 quart
4 quarts = 1 gallon

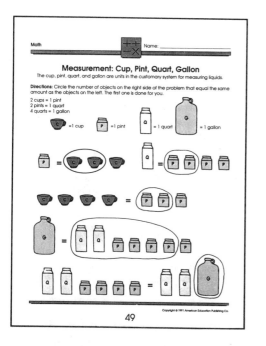

= 1 cup   = 1 pint   = 1 quart   = 1 gallon

49

Measurement: Meters And Kilometers

Meters and kilometers are distance measurements in the metric system. A meter is equal to 100 centimeters. It is a little longer than a yard — 39.37 inches (a yard is 36 inches). A doorknob is about 1 meter from the floor. You can write **m** to stand for meter.

Kilometers are used to measure long distances, such as the distance traveled by a car. There are 1000 meters in a kilometer. A kilometer is equal to about 5/8 of a mile. You can write **km** to stand for kilometer.

Directions: Choose the measure of distance you would use for each object.

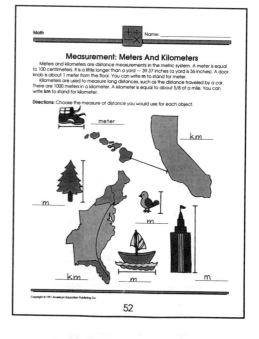

meter   km

m

m

km   m   m

52

81

Measurement: Perimeter, Area, And Volume

The perimeter is the distance around a figure. The area is the number of square units needed to cover a region.

Directions: Find the perimeter and area of each figure.

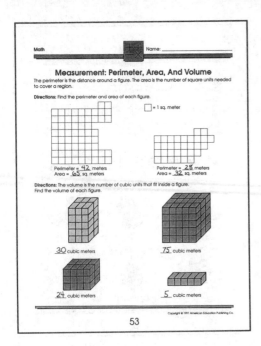

☐ = 1 sq. meter

Perimeter = _42_ meters
Area = _65_ sq. meters

Perimeter = _28_ meters
Area = _32_ sq. meters

Directions: The volume is the number of cubic units that fit inside a figure. Find the volume of each figure.

_30_ cubic meters

_75_ cubic meters

_24_ cubic meters

_5_ cubic meters

53

Measurement: Gram And Kilogram

Grams and kilograms are measurements of weight in the metric system. A gram weighs about 1/28 of an ounce. There are 1000 grams in a kilogram. A kilogram weights about 2.2 pounds.

Directions: Decide whether to use grams or kilograms to measure each of the following.

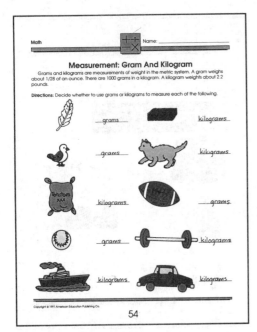

grams

kilograms

grams

kilograms

kilograms

grams

grams

kilograms

kilograms

kilograms

54

Measurements: Milliliter And Liter

Liters and milliliters are units in the metric system for measuring liquids. A milliliter (mL stands for milliliter) equals .0001 liter. Liters (L) measure large amounts of liquid. There are 1000 milliliters in a liter.

Directions: Choose milliliters or liters to measure these liquids.

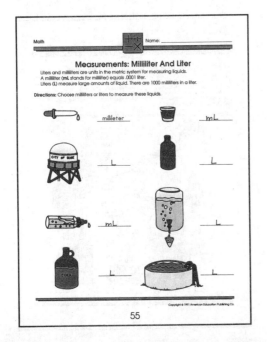

milliliter

_mL_

_L_

_L_

_mL_

_L_

_L_

_L_

55

Temperature: Celsius

Temperature tells us how hot or cold something is. The degree Celsius is used to measure temperature in the metric system. °C stands for degree Celsius.

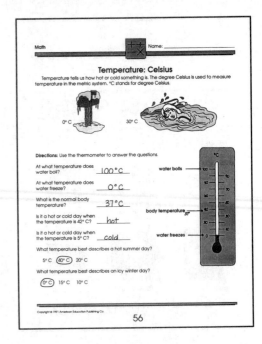

0° C   30° C

Directions: Use the thermometer to answer the questions.

At what temperature does water boil?   _100° C_   water boils

At what temperature does water freeze?   _0° C_

What is the normal body temperature?   _37° C_   body temperature

Is it a hot or cold day when the temperature is 42° C?   _hot_

Is it a hot or cold day when the temperature is 5° C?   _cold_   water freezes

What temperature best describes a hot summer day?

5° C   (40° C)   20° C

What temperature best describes an icy winter day?

(0° C)   15° C   10° C

56

Temperature: Fahrenheit

The degree Fahrenheit is used to measure temperature in the customary system. °F stands for degree Fahrenheit.

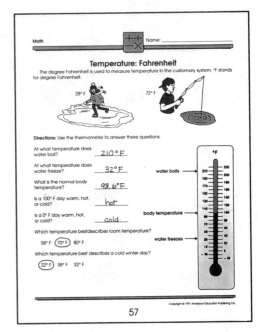

28° F   72° F

Directions: Use the thermometer to answer these questions.

At what temperature does water boil?   _210° F_

At what temperature does water freeze?   _32° F_   water boils

What is the normal body temperature?   _98.6° F_

Is a 100° F day warm, hot, or cold?   _hot_   body temperature

Is a 0° F day warm, hot, or cold?   _cold_

Which temperature bestdescribes room temperature?

58° F   (70° F)   80° F   water freezes

Which temperature best describes a cold winter day?

(22° F)   38° F   32° F

57

Review

Directions: Choose centimeter, meter, or kilometer to measure each of the following.

the height of a tree _meter_   the height of a building _meter_

length of a shoe _centimeter_   length of the school yard _meter_

distance around the earth _kilometer_   distance a plane flies _kilometer_

Directions: Choose grams or kilograms to measure each of the following.

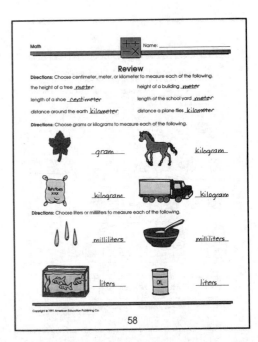

gram

kilogram

kilogram

kilogram

Directions: Choose liters or milliliters to measure each of the following.

milliliters

milliliters

liters

liters

58

Graphs

A graph is a drawing that shows information about changes in number.

Directions: Answer the questions by reading the graphs.

Bar Graph

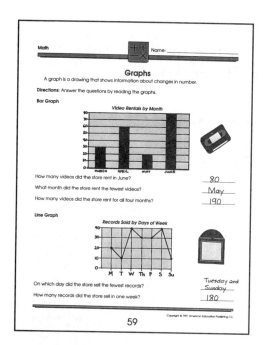

Video Rentals by Month

How many videos did the store rent in June?   **80**

What month did the store rent the fewest videos?   **May**

How many videos did the store rent for all four months?   **190**

Line Graph

Records Sold by Days of Week

On which day did the store sell the fewest records?   **Tuesday and Sunday**

How many records did the store sell in one week?   **180**

59

Geometry: Lines, Rays, Segments

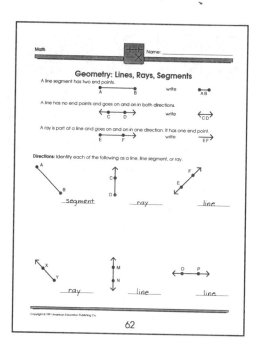

A line segment has two end points.   write $\overline{AB}$

A line has no end points and goes on and on in both directions.   write $\overleftrightarrow{CD}$

A ray is part of a line and goes on and on in one direction. It has one end point.   write $\overrightarrow{EF}$

Directions: Identify each of the following as a line, line segment, or ray.

segment   **ray**   **line**

ray   **line**   **line**

62

Ordered Pairs

An ordered pair is a pair of numbers used to locate a point.

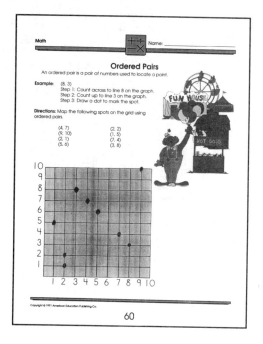

Example: (8, 3)
Step 1: Count across to line 8 on the graph.
Step 2: Count up to line 3 on the graph.
Step 3: Draw a dot to mark the spot.

Directions: Map the following spots on the grid using ordered pairs.

(4, 7)	(2, 2)
(9, 10)	(1, 5)
(2, 1)	(7, 4)
(5, 6)	(3, 8)

60

Geometry: Circles

A circle is a round figure. It is named by its center.
A radius is a line segment from the center to any point on the circle.
A diameter is a line segment with both points on the circle. The diameter always passes through the center of the circle.

Directions: Name the radius, diameter, and circle.

Example:

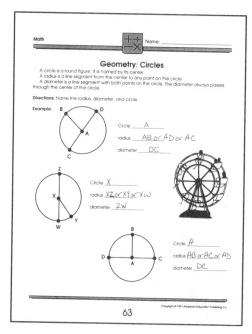

Circle   **A**
radius   **AB or AD or AC**
diameter   **DC**

Circle   **X**
radius   **XZ or XY or XW**
diameter   **ZW**

Circle   **A**
radius   **AB or AC or AD**
diameter   **DC**

63

Geometry: Polygons

A polygon is a closed figure with three or more sides.

Directions: Identify the polygons.

Example:

triangle	square	rectangle	pentagon	hexagon	octagon
3 sides	4 equal sides	4 sides	5 sides	6 sides	8 sides

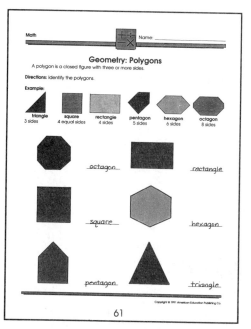

octagon   **rectangle**

square   **hexagon**

pentagon   **triangle**

61

Review

Directions: Complete the graph using the information in the box.

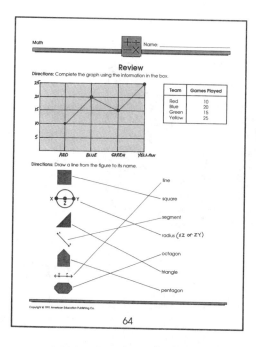

Team	Games Played
Red	10
Blue	20
Green	15
Yellow	25

Directions: Draw a line from the figure to its name.

line

square

segment

radius (XZ or ZY)

octagon

triangle

pentagon

64

83

INTRODUCING
BRIGHTER CHILD™ SOFTWARE!

BRIGHTER CHILD ™ SOFTWARE for Windows

These colorful and exciting programs teach basic skills in an entertaining way. They are based on the best selling BRIGHTER CHILD™ workbooks, written and designed by experts who are also parents. Sound is included to facilitate learning, but it is not nesessary to run these programs. BRIGHTER CHILD™ software has received many outstanding reviews and awards. All Color! Easy to use!

The following programs are each sold separately in a 3.5 disk format.

Reading & Phonics Grade 1	*Reading Grade 2*	*Reading Grade 3*
Math Grade 1	*Math Grade 2*	*Math Grade 3*

CD-ROM Titles!

These new titles combine three grade levels of a subject on one CD-ROM! Each CD contains more than 80 different activities packed with colors and sound.

Reading and Phonics Challenge - CD-ROM Grades 1, 2, 3

Math Challenge - CD-ROM Grades 1, 2, 3

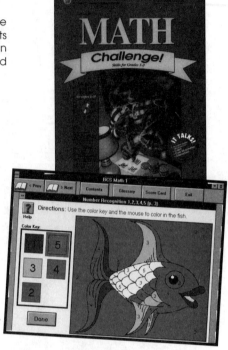

JIM HENSON'S MUPPET™/
BRIGHTER CHILD™ SOFTWARE for Windows™

Based on the best selling Muppet Press™/BRIGHTER CHILD™ Workbooks, these software programs for Windows are designed to teach basic concepts to children in preschool and kindergarten. Children will develop phonics skills and critical and creative thinking skills, and more! No reading is required with a sound card -- the directions are read aloud. The Muppet™ characters are universally known and loved and are recognized as having high educational value.

The following programs are each sold separately in a 3.5 disk format.
Each package contains:

- a program disk with more than 15 full color animated interactive lessons!
- sound is included which facilitates learning.
- Full-color workbook

Beginning Sounds: Phonics	*Letters: Capital & Small*
Same & Different	

CD-ROM Titles

Beginning Reading & Phonics- CD-ROM

This title combines three different MUPPET™/BRIGHTER CHILD™ Software programs -- Beginning Sounds: Phonics, Letters, and Same and Different -- all on one CD-ROM! This valuable software contains more than 50 different activities packed with color, sound, and interactive animation!

Reading & Phonics II- CD-ROM

Three Muppet™ Early Reading Programs on one CD-ROM. Includes *Sorting & Ordering, Thinking Skills,* and *Sound Patterns: More Phonics*

Available at stores everywhere.

OVERVIEW

ENRICHMENT READING is designed to provide children with practice in reading and to increase students' reading abilities. The program consists of six editions, one each for grades 1 through 6. The major areas of reading instruction--word skills, vocabulary, study skills, comprehension, and literary forms--are covered as appropriate at each level.

ENRICHMENT READING provides a wide range of activities that target a variety of skills in each instructional area. The program is unique because it helps children expand their skills in playful ways with games, puzzles, riddles, contests, and stories. The high-interest activities are informative and fun to do.

Home involvement is important to any child's success in school. *ENRICHMENT READING* is the ideal vehicle for fostering home involvement. Every lesson provides specific opportunities for children to work with a parent, a family member, an adult, or a friend.

AUTHORS

Peggy Kaye, the author of *ENRICHMENT READING*, is also an author of *ENRICHMENT MATH* and the author of two parent/teacher resource books, *Games for Reading* and *Games for Math*. Currently, Ms. Kaye divides her time between writing books and tutoring students in reading and math. She has also taught for ten years in New York City public and private schools.

WRITERS

Timothy J. Baehr is a writer and editor of instructional materials on the elementary, secondary, and college levels. Mr. Baehr has also authored an award-winning column on bicycling and a resource book for writers of educational materials.

Cynthia Benjamin is a writer of reading instructional materials, television scripts, and original stories. Ms. Benjamin has also tutored students in reading at the New York University Reading Institute.

Russell Ginns is a writer and editor of materials for a children's science and nature magazine. Mr. Ginn's speciality is interactive materials, including games, puzzles, and quizzes.

WHY ENRICHMENT READING?

Enrichment and parental involvement are both crucial to children's success in school, and educators recognize the important role work done at home plays in the educational process. Enrichment activities give children opportunities to practice, apply, and expand their reading skills, while encouraging them to think while they read. *ENRICHMENT READING* offers exactly this kind of opportunity. Each lesson focuses on an important reading skill and involves children in active learning. Each lesson will entertain and delight children.

When childen enjoy their lessons and are involved in the activities, they are naturally alert and receptive to learning. They understand more. They remember more. All children enjoy playing games, having contests, and solving puzzles. They like reading interesting stories, amusing stories, jokes, and riddles. Activities such as these get children involved in reading. This is why these kinds of activities form the core of *ENRICHMENT READING*.

Each lesson consists of two parts. Children complete the first part by themselves. The second part is completed together with a family member, an adult, or a friend. *ENRICHMENT READING* activities do not require people at home to teach reading. Instead, the activities involve everyone in enjoyable reading games and interesting language experiences.

ENRICHMENT ANSWER KEY
Math Grade 4

Page 65 : answers will vary. Possible answers given.
1. $2+2+2-3-3=0$
2. $2+2-3=1$
3. $3+3-2-2=2$
4. $3+2-2=3$

Page 66 : answers will vary

Page 67 : answers will vary

Page 68: answers will vary

ENRICHMENT ANSWER KEY
Math Grade 4

Page 69 : answers will vary

Page 70 : answers will vary

Page 71 : answers will vary

Page 72 : answers will vary. Possible answers given.

1. Remove 2 toothpicks.
   Leave 3 squares.

2. Remove 4 toothpicks.
   Leave 2 squares.

3. Remove 4 toothpicks.
   Leave 4 squares.

4. Remove 5 toothpicks.
   Leave 4 squares.

5. Remove 8 toothpicks.
   Leave 5 squares.

6. Remove 4 toothpicks.
   Leave 5 squares.